PENGUIN BOOKS

Shoes Were for Sunday

Molly Weir was born in 1910 and grew up in Glasgow. Best known for her role as the character Hazel McWitch in the BBC TV series *Renta-ghost*, she appeared prolifically on TV, radio and in film. *Shoes Were for Sunday* received great acclaim when first published in 1970, and became a bestseller. She died in 2004, leaving the proceeds of her estate, including the royalties from sales of this book, to the poor and elderly of her beloved Springburn in Glasgow.

Shoes Were for Sunday

MOLLY WEIR

PENGUIN BOOKS

PENGUIN BOOKS

Published by the Penguin Group
Penguin Books Ltd, 80 Strand, London WC2R ORL, England
Penguin Group (USA) Inc., 375 Hudson Street, New York, New York 10014, USA
Penguin Group (Canada), 90 Eglinton Avenue East, Suite 700, Toronto, Ontario,
Canada M4P 2Y3 (a division of Pearson Penguin Canada Inc.)
Penguin Ireland, 25 St Stephen's Green, Dublin 2, Ireland (a division of Penguin Books Ltd)
Penguin Group (Australia), 250 Camberwell Road,
Camberwell, Victoria 3124, Australia (a division of Pearson Australia Group Pty Ltd)
Penguin Books India Pvt Ltd, 11 Community Centre,
Panchsheel Park, New Delhi – 110 017, India
Penguin Group (NZ), 67 Apollo Drive, Rosedale, Auckland 0632, New Zealand
(a division of Pearson New Zealand Ltd)
Penguin Books (South Africa) (Pty) Ltd, 24 Sturdee Avenue,
Rosebank, Johannesburg 2196, South Africa

Penguin Books Ltd, Registered Offices: 80 Strand, London WC2R ORL, England

www.penguin.com

First published by Hutchinson & Co. (Publishers) Ltd 1970
Reissued by Pan Books Ltd 1973
Published in Penguin Books 2012
002

Set in 12.5/14.75 pt Garamond MT Std
Typeset by Jouve (UK), Milton Keynes
Printed in England by Clays Ltd, St Ives plc

ISBN: 978-0-241-95792-9

www.greenpenguin.co.uk

MIX
Paper from
responsible sources
FSC C018179

Penguin Books is committed to a sustainable
future for our business, our readers and our planet.
This book is made from Forest Stewardship
Council™ certified paper.

ALWAYS LEARNING   **PEARSON**

Dedicated to Grannie, and to her daughter,
who was my mother

'What strange, mysterious links enchain the heart, to regions where the morn of life was spent.'

JAMES GRAHAME

One

Somehow I was never awake at the precise moment when Grannie came into bed. One minute I was drowsily gazing at the gas mantle, blinking my lashes against its soft radiance and making rainbows with my flickering eyelids and its glowing globe, and the next moment it was dark and Grannie was pulling the blankets round her, and easing herself into the hollow in front of me. As I cooried in closer, to keep my share of the bedclothes, she would reach out a hand to push my knees down. 'Your banes are like sticks,' she would complain. 'Streetch them doon noo. They're that sherp, they're cuttin' intae auld Grannie's back.' Sleepily, obediently, I would straighten out my legs, and I would drift off with a drowsy smile as I prodded with a small hand my offending knees. How could Grannie think they were sharp enough to hurt her? I wondered. They felt soft and ordinary enough to me. But then I was only three years old and Grannie was, oh maybe a hundred, for, after all, she was my mother's mother, and my mother was twenty-one, for she had told us so when we asked her.

I couldn't remember a time when I hadn't slept in the hurley bed with Grannie. This was a bed on casters, which 'hurled' under the big recess bed out of sight during the day, and was hidden tidily out of sight behind the bed-pawn, ready to be pulled out at a touch whenever it was my bedtime. It was only about a foot off the floor, so that it could be hurled away fully made up with its sheets and pillows and blankets, and was probably made by a neighbour who was a handyman joiner, and who grasped at once the necessity for using every inch of space in a room and kitchen which had to accommodate five people.

There was my grannie, my mother, my two brothers and myself. Away, way back I had a dream-like memory of a man who refused to pick me up and carry me when we had been out visiting one bitterly cold Sunday, and it was very late, and we couldn't find a tramcar. 'Give her a carry,' my mother's voice said. 'She's only a baby.' 'She can walk,' came the man's voice. 'There's nothing wrong with her legs.' There was no spoiling for me. That must have been my father. A father who lived only long enough to sire three children. Four if you count the little sister who died in infancy, and whom he quickly followed, leaving my mother to bring the three of us up without anybody's help except that given by Grannie. Grannie gave up her own wee single end, and came to live with us. I never missed my father. For, filling every corner of my world was Grannie. From the minute I opened my eyes in the hurley bed in the morning, she tormented me, disciplined me, taught me, laughed at me, loved me, and tied me to her for ever, although I didn't know it at the time.

We called our room and kitchen a 'house', for we'd never heard of the word 'flat' when I was a wee girl. It was in a red sandstone tenement, which we thought far nicer than the dull grey tenements farther up the road. In some mysterious way some closes were smarter than others. The Cooperative close at No 290 was considered really classy. For one thing there were no children, and instead of painted dark green walls inside the close, like the other tenements, this one had tiles which were the envy of every other tenement wife, for they could be wiped clean at the touch of a cloth, and this sparkling cleanliness awed us with its rich look. This back court, too, was different from our ordinary earth one, for it was concreted all over, and the wall which divided it from our lesser courts was higher than ours, and not a railing was missing. This rigid iron barrier was useless in keeping out the rest of us children from the teeming tenements. Although we were fully aware it was forbidden territory, every now and then, just to test our courage, we would go tearing through the splendid tiled close and invade the concreted back court. We would stot our balls in an ecstasy of delight to see how high they would bounce off this marvellous concrete, then throw them against the walls of the posh tenement itself. Then, freedom from punishment going to our heads, we would go mad and start yelling at the tops of our voices, without rhyme or reason, 'Come up for yer dinner, ya red-heided sinner, cauld totties an' herrin'.'

At that a window would be thrown up, and an

outraged face would appear. This was the policeman's house, and we shivered at our own daring in arousing his wife's wrath. 'Go back to your own back courts,' she called out furiously, in a much more polite accent than our own mothers', we noted, 'and stop yelling.' Yelling? Who was yelling? We were only singing. We were intensely curious about this woman, who had no children. We gazed at her, mesmerized, trying to imagine her quiet house with only herself and the policeman to keep her company.

I remember one day when I was about seven years old she actually called me up from where I was playing in the next back court and asked me to run to the butcher's and get half a pound of mince for her. I was startled to find she ate ordinary mince like us. When I went back to hand it over she asked me in, instead of keeping me on the doorstep like all the other mothers, who certainly didn't encourage us to race over their clean linoleum with our dirty feet. I stood stiffly in the middle of the floor, frightened to move in case I'd break anything, and astounded at the neatness and tidiness of it all. No toys. No papers. No shiny American cloth stretched over the table to keep it safe from spilt tea or gravy. Instead, unbelievably, a polished table with a vase of flowers on top. My eyes darted round the room, taking everything in, and I was quite dazzled by its splendour, and I felt a singing in my ears at its quietness. I'd never been in a house before which wasn't noisy with lively children. She gave me a piece of gingerbread which was so generously spread with salt butter that the richness was too much for me and I couldn't eat it. When half a pound of margarine had to last five of us as long as it could possibly be stretched, and the paper scraped to get the last tiny piece, you weren't used to your teeth meeting a thick layer of butter. But I wouldn't have dreamt of wasting it. I ran home with it to Grannie and she scraped off the thick top layer and prudently put it aside for her own tea later. She loved this butter, which she seldom got, but I, brought up on the cheaper margarine, thought it had a funny taste and gladly let Grannie enjoy this beanfeast.

Grannie could see I was full of my privileged peep at the inside of the policeman's house, and I daresay she was quite curious herself, for nobody else on our stair had ever got over the door. 'Grannie,' I said excitedly, 'she's got a house like a palace. Everything's shining! Dae ye know whit she was daein' when ah went in? She was polishin' the kettle, Grannie. The kettle! No' the brass kettle for the mantelpiece. The kettle that sits on the range. And it would juist get durty again as soon as she pit it oan the fire.' 'Och well, lassie,' said Grannie comfortably, 'she's got nae weans, you see, and she disnae ken whit to be at tae pass the time.'

Ever afterwards in my mind childlessness and sparkling tidiness went together, and when I passed the policeman's wife in the street after that she seemed to belong to another species, and I'd follow her in imagination into her quiet neat house, with never a raucous child to disturb its serenity. And I never made a noise in her back court again.

Old Grannie's down our stair was another house which fascinated me for much the same reason. Her children were all grown up long ago, and the silence and orderliness were such a contrast to our lively, bustling, noisy house that I needed no coaxing to go down to see if she needed any messages. She was a very old lady, even older than my grannie. She had a thin pink face, snow-white hair, was thin as a whippet, and she moved so slowly I felt sure she was frightened her bones would break if she hurried. She came from Ayrshire, and her accent was different from ours, and she called a saucer a 'flet', which I found highly diverting. She had photograph albums with pictures which went right back to her childhood, and it was my delight to pore over them by the hour, asking, 'And was this your husband, Grannie,' for I knew it only needed that question for her to gaze dreamily into the coals and tell me about how she had gone to her first dance in the country at the age of fifteen, and how this handsome man with the moustache and side-whiskers had come over to her and asked her to dance. At the end of the reel he had thrown his bag of sweeties into her lap and said, 'You're for me,' and they were married when she was sixteen. The speed and directness of this courtship took my breath away. 'But did you *love* him, Grannie,' I would ask every time this story was told. I passionately wanted her to have some opinion on the matter. 'Aye

I suppose I did, lassie,' she would smile. 'But, you see, ah wis a ferm servant, and in those days you were only too pleased to get a guid man, and a hoose o' yer ain, so you didnae speir at yersel' too much aboot whether or no' ye liked him. And in oor village it was aye the man who did the seekin'.' As I gazed at the solemn bewhiskered face in the photograph I found it hard to imagine this dull man had ever done anything so romantic as sweep Grannie off her feet at the age of fifteen. Nevertheless, Grannie was only waiting now to join him in heaven, and under the bed she had a wooden chest containing her shroud and a cotton 'mutch', and even the pennies to cover her eyes, and a white bandage to tie round her mouth.

My mother was unwittingly roped in to help to fill this wooden burial chest with the final item. She had spent the whole of one precious lunch hour going into every haberdashery in Springburn searching for a cotton 'mutch', which this old grannie had asked her to buy for her, thinking the old lady was feeling the cold and wanted it there and then. When she dashed in in triumph, having found it in the very last shop, she was furious when Grannie pulled out the chest and said with satisfaction, 'Aye, that's the lot noo. I can go any time.' As my mother bolted her sausages before rushing back to her work in the Railways, she said to my grannie, 'Fancy that old rascal making me flee all over Springburn for something she'll no' want till she's deid. And here was me thinkin' ah wis doin' her a good turn, and keepin' her heid warm on these cauld nights.' My own grannie laughed, 'Weel, so you have done her a guid turn. She'll sleep faur better noo, kennin' her burial trousseau is complete.' In spite of herself, my mother had to laugh. But I didn't laugh. For I sometimes went down to sleep with this old lady to keep her company in the winter, and I didn't like the thought of sleeping on a bed with a shroud and burial garments in a fearsome box underneath.

All our neighbours were a source of great interest to me. I didn't see them as an assortment of shabbily dressed women struggling against heavy odds to make ends meet, and keep dirt at bay. I was vividly aware of their peculiarities, and absorbed in their lives. There was our red-faced upstairs neighbour, with her five pale children and her dull quiet husband, who hardly opened his mouth. She was the terror of the stair. We could tell at a glance when she was in ferocious mood, as likely as not to give you a swipe in the passing just for staring at her. She was a huge woman, and I used to shiver with fright when the sound of yelling and screaming in her house above our head told me she was giving the children another walloping. Her violence terrified me, and I never dreamed the day would dawn when she would become a semi-paralysed invalid, worn out by her own wild temper. Maybe she had high blood pressure or some awful secret illness, for we never associated health with behaviour. You were either a targe or you weren't, and there was an end of it.

There was a dirty woman in a nearby close, quiet and self-effacing, who stank to high heaven and we took the smell with the personality, but gave her a wide berth just the same. I was sternly forbidden ever to borrow a comb from any of her children in case I'd borrow a few beasts at the same time. My mother had vowed that when she had been speaking to her she'd been horrified to see the beasts running round the wool which tied this woman's specs to her ears! I made an excuse to go to her door, and, staring fixedly at the wool holding the specs, noted without as much as a shudder that my mother was right. It was no exaggeration.

I was usually far too wise to repeat any of the remarks overheard in our kitchen, but once I got carried away by what I thought was Grannie's praise of a chum's mother who had a particularly explosive laugh. I burst out admiringly, 'Oh, Mrs D., laugh like that again. My grannie says you've a laugh like a hen cackling.' Grannie seized me by the ear the minute I came in from play and demanded to know why I'd been so silly as to cause trouble like this, for of course Mrs D. had been furious. Somehow I just couldn't make Grannie understand that I thought it was a compliment. If I had been able to laugh like a hen cackling I'd have been delighted with my cleverness. Grannie sighed, for she knew that one of my proudest party pieces was imitating a chimpanzee, walk, grimace, shrieks and all, and I had to be threatened with walloping before I'd promise never to do it again.

There was even a dandy in the tenement, who donned yellow chamois gloves when he went out courting another woman, not his wife. She, poor thing, couldn't stop his amorous ways, but his mother-in-law told me fiercely, 'He's a rotter. He's lived on the steps o' the jile a' his life.' How could he live on the steps of the jail, I wondered, and still live up our stair? She also told me darkly that he'd even broken into a harem during the war, and had been lucky not to have been shot for it. A harem! What was so terrible about that? I would have liked to have seen inside a harem myself, and gazed upon all those concubines, a word which had intrigued me ever since I first read it in the Bible.

There was a wee skinny woman, so poor that she actually was glad to do our washing for us for half a crown, for my mother was too exhausted after her heavy work in the Railways to do this herself. This wee creature crept down to the warmth of our fire every single night in life. She never opened her mouth, but rocked silently back and forth, sipping the tea Grannie always had ready for her. Once when my auntie came to stay with us on a visit from Australia, and could stand this woman's silent presence not a minute longer, she jokingly sprang up and shouted to the wee washerwoman, 'What the devil are you making all the noise about?' The wee creature got such a shock she leaped to her feet, spilling tea all over the fireside, and rushed from the house, and never came back until Auntie had safely left for Australia again. My mother was mad, because we got no more washings done for us all the time Auntie was with us.

But our very favourite neighbours, for us children I mean, were the newly married ones. When they came to our tenements they seemed so fresh, and lively, and young, after all the workworn mothers we knew. They sang at their work in their newly furnished kitchens. They didn't mind us perching on the window-ledges of their ground-floor tenement rooms and watching their every move. They showed off a bit as they worked, and we loved their exaggerated movements as they lifted kettles and polished their brasses. And they always had babies for us to take out in the big enveloping shawls which wrapped baby and baby-minder in a safe, warm cocoon. There were no prams in the tenements. A pram was as impossible in our economy as a Rolls-Royce. But if babies didn't always get enough to eat, they always had the warmth and comfort of being wrapped close to a loving body.

I was so small, nobody would entrust me to carry their baby in this way, although I was occasionally allowed to hold one on my lap. It was my life's ambition to be trusted to take one of those babies out in a shawl. At last one newly wed mother yielded to my non-stop coaxing. Trembling, I took the baby in my left arm, while the mother wrapped the big grey shawl firmly round the baby, then across my back, under my right arm, and tucked the ends safely below my right hand. Alas, she didn't notice she'd left an end of the shawl hanging down at the back, and I'd not walked a dozen yards into the back courts proudly carrying my precious burden when I tripped and went rolling over and over in the dirt. I never let go the baby, I'm proud to say, and it didn't seem unduly disturbed as it rolled over and over with me. But the mother nearly had a fit and came screaming from the house, seized the baby from me, and had a terrifying bout of hysterics with the sheer relief of finding it was still alive and no bones broken. That ended my career as a baby-minder. The whole back court had seen me, and I was disgraced. I rushed up to the swings at the top of Springburn to forget my misery, and was soon able to stop my trembling unhappiness as I flew round and round on the joy-wheel, and soared higher and higher on the big swings.

And yet, much as I enjoyed the excitement of the young neighbours, the face which comes and looks at me gravely through the years is the face of Mrs McCorbie.

How is this? I wonder. I've a feeling that some people have a quality about them which singles them out for attention wherever fate chooses to place them, and however humbly they work out their destinies. They're the sort of people whose lives fascinate novelists, for they've an out-of-the-ordinary ambience which makes their slightest action memorable.

Born into an artistic background, they'd attract painters and poets to sing their praises, but even when found among the working classes they somehow manage to triumph over the drabness of their surroundings and find a dignity which lifts them above the commonplace.

At least, that's how it strikes me. For why, among so many, should I remember Mrs McCorbie with such an anguished pang?

We were very proud that she should have singled us out for her friendship, because she had the stiff reserve of the very poor who can't mix freely for fear of getting caught up in an expenditure which was quite beyond her. There wasn't the tiniest margin in Mrs McCorbie's budget which she could spare for all the hundred and one little social occasions which made up our lives. A penny for the hospitals, a penny for a wreath, a penny towards a present for wee Cathie who was dying in hospital of tuberculosis, and so on, and so on. Each sum minute in itself, but quite beyond the reach of Mrs McCorbie, whose every penny was painfully earned and had to do the work of three.

She was only too aware of her poverty, and the easy-going ways of others in the same state were beyond her, and we were her only friends.

It was never mentioned, but years later I understood that her husband, who had brought Mrs McCorbie from the Highlands to the big city where work was plentiful, had later deserted her and their children for another woman. I don't suppose he'd ever seen blonde dyed hair or make-up before he came to Glasgow, or been aware that his own splendid physique was so attractive to women. Wife, children, responsibilities, were forgotten and he vanished to be seen no more.

Mrs McCorbie, stunned and bewildered, had been too proud to try to trace him to make him provide for the children. Instead, after the first numbness had worn off, she faced the grim necessity of providing food and clothing and, most urgent of all, of meeting the monthly demands for rent. They could survive most things if they could just keep the roof over their heads.

She couldn't leave home to look for work, for the children were still very young and needed constant attention and nobody in our tenements had time to take another family under their wing; they had children of their own which took all their energies and patience. No, it had to be something she could do within the four walls of her own living-room. Her eye, I imagine, fell on the sewing machine she had brought from her Highland home, and she had an inspiration. She would take in sewing. But not for the neighbours, oh no. She wouldn't be dependent on them for her livelihood. Anyway, she had to be paid as the work was done, and she knew she could never ask neighbours for payment if they were careless about their debts.

She had heard somewhere that factories sometimes employed home workers. So, dressing in her neat black coat, and pulling a felt hat over her mass of coiled black hair, she went to the only factory she knew, a large warehouse in the city where her husband had occasionally bought shirts. They were willing to let her stitch the collars and cuffs on their shirts for the handsome sum of a farthing per shirt. She was to collect a pile of unfinished shirts, loose collars and cuffs each morning, and return them the following morning, when she could collect a fresh batch. There was no limit to the amount she could have – it was entirely up to her how much she earned.

So her life of slavery to the machine began.

This all happened before I was born, and by the time I was toddling up and down the tenement stairs I accepted as part of the pattern of my life the whirring sound of the machine, like a gigantic bumble-bee, constantly buzzing in the house of Mrs McCorbie.

Her one treasured relaxation was the early-morning visit to our house to see my grannie. We lived immediately above her and it was my mother's furious denunciation of the scoundrelly Mr McCorbie that drew this wordlessly suffering woman to us in the first place. She herself didn't utter a word in self-pity or anger against her husband – her hurt went too deep for that – but in my mother's rage Mrs McCorbie sensed a warmth and a friendship for herself that she needed desperately at that time. Her reserve melted. She crept out from behind her shut front door and the morning visits helped her face her daily struggle. It was quite a little ritual. She would wait until the light tread of Grannie's footsteps overhead assured her that she wasn't too early, and her soft tap on the door was hospitably answered by Grannie's half-surprised, 'Oh come in, Mrs McCorbie,' as though the visit was a delightful impulse. She never accepted Grannie's invitation to sit down – that would have implied a real call – but always stood by the dresser, almost silent, listening with a quiet smile to Grannie's chatter and watching her brisk, busy movements as she made the porridge for us children and set the table for breakfast. As she watched and listened, she subconsciously swung her house keys round her finger on a ring, and it's one of the most vivid memories of my early childhood, slowly emerging from sleep to the accompanying tinkle of Mrs McCorbie's keys, and then, as awareness grew, enjoying the steady murmur of the voices, pitched on a comforting low tone so that we might not be disturbed before it was necessary. I would glance through sleepy lashes, noting with pleasure the heavy coil of jet-black hair at the base of Mrs McCorbie's neck, the soft brown eyes and the pale skin, and become slightly hypnotized by the firelight winking and dancing in rosy reflection off the jingling keys she held.

By the time I was about six years old, her children were all out at work, but still she sewed eternally at those dreadful shirts. My mother was bitter in her denunciation of the three ingrate McCorbie children. 'Take after their father, every one of them,' she would exclaim. 'They're not fit to brush their mother's shoes, and look at them!' I looked, and saw two haughty girls and a strapping boy. Each went their separate ways, neither helping with the housework nor giving their mother enough money to make life easier for her. Now that they were grown up, all their meagre wages were required for dress and amusement.

As the whirr of the machine reached us during supper, my mother would start up in indignation. 'Listen to her, slaving away at that machine, and it's nearly ten o'clock at night.' I was startled by the word 'slaving', because Grannie was reading *Uncle Tom's Cabin* to me, and I thought slaves were all black. 'Maybe it's her black hair,' I thought to myself, 'that makes her a slave.'

Now that her family were out all day, Mrs McCorbie had nobody to run messages for her, and one day I heard her asking in her soft Highland voice if Grannie thought I might be willing to do this for her. 'Willing!' said Grannie at once. 'Of course she'll be willing.' There was no question of consulting me, for laziness was something which was simply not recognized in our family. The simple facts were that Mrs McCorbie needed a messenger, and I had plenty of free time after I'd got Grannie's messages in, so I might as well be useful as idle. Grannie knew that I was a bundle of energy, and if that energy could be used to help poor Mrs McCorbie, so much the better for everyone.

I presented myself at Mrs McCorbie's door after school, and we had a thrilling consultation about payment. It had never entered my head that I would be paid, but she gravely said she was willing to pay me a penny a day for full use of my shopping services when Grannie had finished with me. 'Full use' meant the shopping hours weren't to be confined to after four o'clock school, but I might be asked to go in the morning, or even at lunch-time in emergency. I eagerly accepted, and then there was the delicious choice of having my penny each day, or sixpence on a Saturday. I considered the matter carefully. There didn't seem much point in having a penny each day unless I were going to spend it, and that wasn't really fair to my other chums, for nobody else could afford sweeties during the week. The total wealth of the others seldom went beyond threepence or fourpence. If I took the whole sixpence on a Saturday, why I'd be able to save. I could put something past every week for Christmas and birthday presents and for the summer holidays. I felt dizzy with power. It was the start of a fortune. A silver sixpence weekly it was.

As my mother later said, I was Mrs McCorbie's body and soul for that sixpence. She used to knock on the ceiling when she wanted me, and even if I were raising the teacup to my lips I'd lay it down untasted when I heard the knock, and I would be at her door in a flash, ready to run the forgotten errand. Not that Mrs McCorbie wanted such instant obedience, but I had a high sense of responsibility towards my employer, and, with the wisdom of the poor, I knew what that sixpence meant to her.

We didn't speak very much to each other, I remember. Poor, over-worked people have little leisure for mere conversation, but I think she liked me coming to her door each day to see if I were wanted, and occasionally I was allowed to rummage through the drawers and play with the empty cotton reels, and to build lovely little houses with them. There was a silent companionship between us, and, of course, for me she had the added fascination of being 'a slave', for I never forgot my mother's description.

She saw less and less of her children. They'd come home from work, swallow their food, and be off again. One very hot summer night, when I was about ten, the youngest daughter came running into the back court where we were playing. She was white to the lips and trembling. 'My mother is dead,' she said. My heart gave a terrible lurch, for I had never met death until this time. I looked at the soft skies, and then at the bright eyes of my playmates and couldn't believe it wasn't some awful nightmare. The bigger girls crowded round me, for they knew our family were on intimate terms with Mrs McCorbie, but I crept away, dazed and shaken by the shock. I hadn't the usual childish sense of importance because I was close to the central figure in this drama – I felt sick and wanted to go home.

I stole quietly past Mrs McCorbie's door, and it was terrible not to hear the whirr of the machine when it was still daylight, for she always worked until the last light faded from the sky. Now there was silence. They sent for my mother, and when she went down she found Mrs McCorbie slumped over her machine, her hands still holding shirt and collar, ready to join them under the needle. The pins had fallen from her hair, and it hung, long and black, to her knees and my mother told me later that she looked like some Highland heroine from a painting, with her pale face and flowing magnificent hair.

Nobody knew where to find the two older children. In their careless fashion they hadn't bothered to tell anyone where they were going. This seemed terrible to us, for, like most of the children of the tenements, we were never allowed out of the house without our mothers knowing exactly where we could be found. We were also left in no doubt as to the hour we were expected to be home.

But the McCorbie children came and went as they pleased. I wondered how long it had been since they had even noticed the little figure bent so uncomplainingly over the machine. I knew I was going to miss her much more than they would. She had been my first employer. Never again would I see the dark eyes approving my speed as I returned, panting, with a little bit of shopping. Never again experience the warm glow of the dignity of service, as she pressed the silver sixpence into my hand for a week's work well done.

I knew a stab of agony as I anticipated the quiet emptiness which would lie behind the McCorbie door from now on, as I passed it on my way up and down-stairs. No more knocks on the ceiling for my services. And, worst of all, no more wakening to the firelight and the jingle of keys against the gentle murmur of a Highland voice mingling with Grannie's.

Two

Like children the world over, we followed an unwritten pattern for our games. One minute we'd be playing peever, which was our name for hop-scotch, and the greatest thing in the world then was to hop skilfully from bed to bed without touching the chalked line, sending the marble disc or peever into the next bed with poised toe; and then, for no apparent reason, we were all hunting out our girds. The gird or hoop season was starting and we didn't want to miss a minute. I can still see my mother's wrath as her snowy bedspread was pushed aside, while we three children groped under the bed for our girds and cleeks. The cleeks were the metal batons we used to control the gird's movements. The pastime was one usually reserved for boys, but as a special concession to my enthusiasm and my flying limbs, I was allowed to join the runners.

There were usually about six of us setting off at one time. An assortment of metal circles leaned against our legs as we waited for the last one to arrive, and we dirled negligently with the cleeks as we listened to the leader outlining the course for that night.

'Noo, it's roon' the buildin' the night first of all. Then

ower the park, doon past the power station, alang the canal bank, an' back by the road.'

'Right.'

With wild skirls and leapings we were off, girds spinning smoothly in front, eyes watchful for a break in the rhythm, cleek ready to administer sharp encouragement at the exact moment of metal wobbling, feet trotting in unbroken pattern as we raced along.

There were tricky moments with bumpy cobblestones, but we experts knew just when to apply the cleek to keep all steady and sweetly running. The menace of tramlines at a complex crossing would have to be met, and cleek, eyes, feet and brain worked at lightning speed to manoeuvre the gird so that one would not fall behind the crowd.

The gird was a magic carpet carrying us into odd and sometimes forbidden corners of the town, and there was an unholy joy in speeding along the canal banks and over the bridges down into the heart of the city, where tolerant policemen waved us through the busy crossings. We must have run miles on these races, and the exercise and caller air filled us with wild exhilaration.

I suppose traffic must have been lighter, for it's a fact that none of us met calamity on our wild outings, and the worst that befell any of us was a broken gird. When this happened the race was abandoned, and we all dawdled back together, to keep the unfortunate owner company, but we didn't really mind this, for a broken gird entailed a visit to the smiddy, and this was a never-palling thrill.

As we drew near the smiddy, we would break into a trot, clattering up the hill, swinging through the hole in the fence which took us slithering down the brae right to the smiddy door, there to cluster in an excited circle watching big Sanny pounding a live, glowing shoe into shape.

He made those horseshoes for stock-piling, but sometimes there would be a horse waiting to be shod, and we stood tense with admiration of Sanny's skill and daring as he hammered and pared, ignoring the wild gleam in the horse's eye as he drove the shoe home.

And then it would be our turn. With one mighty arm Sanny worked the bellows which transformed the smouldering glow of the furnace into a roaring inferno. The gird would be thrust in, heated, and laid on the anvil, and with a few tremendous smacks of the hammer which sent the sparks flying, the fracture was mended.

A quick plunge of the red-hot metal into a bucket of water, a hiss and a cloud of steam, and the job was finished. A penny changed hands, and surely better entertainment was never provided for such a trifling sum.

Trace-horses were a familiar sight in my childhood, and one of the great dramas of our streets in winter-time was when one of those huge creatures slithered on the icy cobbles and went crashing to the ground. A silent crowd would gather round the still form as it lay inert, and I used to be stirred by the power that flowed from their watchfulness, heads bent forward, intent, willing the passive beast to rise.

A child's voice would query wonderingly, 'How can it no get up?', to be answered in deeper tones, 'It's feart it slips again, son. It makes them awfu' nervous once they slide an' clatter doon wi' the frost.'

The carter, cap pushed back to allow free movement for a perplexed scratch, would watch his charge anxiously. 'Come on, Jock,' he would cluck encouragingly. 'Come on noo, gi'es a good try. Up ye come.'

The beast would gather itself for a tremendous effort, and suddenly, every muscle springing to violent activity, eyes rolling and flashing wildly, it would rear in thunderous eruption, sending sparks flying as its hooves struck the cobbles, and the crowd would draw convulsively back in quick alarm in case it should fall among them.

With a slither and a crash it would fall down again in failure, quivering and quiet once more, only the fearful wildness in the eyes betraying the helpless fear that it was trapped and would never rise again.

'Nothing else fur it, mate,' somebody would shout, 'you'll have to loosen it oot o' the shafts.'

The carter had tried to avoid this labour, but he recognized the inevitable, and with elaborate ritual and willing hands to assist, every strap and buckle would be loosened till the animal lay free, only himself to raise now, and no shackling cart to impede his efforts.

A few men would place themselves at strategic points to lend a hand to steady the animal when at the next or the next attempt it had gained its feet, and eager arms thrust forward to keep the beast erect and balanced, while they avoided the danger of plunging head and flying feet.

A cheer would rise from the rest of us as the drama drew to a close, and the huge trembling creature was harnessed to his cart once more.

The men would stroll off, pleased and satisfied at having helped at an event which needed their manhood and their strength, and we children would dash up to the high road to watch the horse clattering away into the distance, past Sanny's smiddy, away into the town.

The high road not only provided a marvellous grandstand view of everything going on underneath on the main thoroughfare, it was also our adventure playground. It provided games and contests of skill quite different from those to be found in the back courts, and we loved it.

On summer evenings as it grew cooler and we became tired of the joys of taking bottles of water and jeely pieces up to the public park, or satiated with the thrills of hunting for 'baggies' which disappointingly died almost as soon as they'd been fished from the pond, somebody would say, 'Whit aboot the high road?' We actually said 'hirode', for we didn't know it was two words and that it meant a road higher than the main road.

In swift consent we'd wheel in that direction, like

migratory birds, each determined to be there first. The one to reach and touch the end pole first was leader for the rest of the evening's playtime. Somehow it was always evening when we thought of pole slides. The leader, having established his right, was obeyed without question. His was the heady power which decided which poles we'd patronize, or whether we would do any sliding at all. We happily fell in with his most fantastic plans, made just as the spirit moved him.

The tall poles were spaced at regular intervals along the main road, and actually carried the overhead wires for the tramcar trolleys, but their tops towered challengingly near to the railings which topped the high wall behind them. These railings were really a safety barrier on the outside perimeter of the high road pavement to protect the heedless from toppling over into the street below. We thought they'd been placed there entirely for our delight, and to us they were the narrow entrance to our adventurous slides on the poles.

This road on such a high level excited us, and we would first of all peep down at the main road, shuddering with pleasurable fear. 'Whit a terrible depth up!' somebody would breathe, and we felt brave as any mountaineer scaling impossible heights. Then, one at a time, the biggest going first to give the smaller ones courage, we'd squeeze our bodies through the narrow railings, reach out, clasp the narrow standard, and with an ecstatic rush slide down to the pavement so far below. A moment's pause to recover from the exhilaration of that breathless slide, then we'd tear round the foot of the hill, and back to the railings again, and so the game went on till bedtime. Sometimes a plump little tummy would stick for a second on its way through. 'Oh, gi'es a shove, ah'm *stuck*!', and the victim's eyes popped with terror. With a mighty shove from the rest of us queuing up behind, he would be released, and the following slide was all the sweeter for the risk that had been involved.

The first two poles were the only ones the younger children ventured to use, because as the gradient rose, the slide to the ground became longer. But when we were very small it was a thrilling occasion when some of the bigger boys joined us. We knew they'd only come to show off, but it was exciting all the same, and we rushed after them as though they were Pied Pipers. They'd swagger past our poles until they reached the very highest, which stood right at the crest of the road. With narrowed eyes they surveyed the hazards and then, because they were too large to squeeze through the railings, actually swung themselves over the top, paused for a second on the supporting stonework, launched themselves at the pole, and skimmed swiftly to the pavement. Timidly we would lean forward, noses pressed to the railings, and follow their rapid progress to the ground. How sickeningly far away it seemed.

They jeered at us, the bigger boys, but when one of our band looked as if he would attempt this death-defying slide there and then, a large hand would hold him back. 'Naw naw, son, look, your erms have to be as long as mine or you'd never be able to grab the pole when you jumped.' And he would hold out an arm and gravely measure the childish arm against it, and prove to us all that bravery wasn't enough. It seemed the wildest optimism to think *we* would ever be big enough or daring enough to attempt such hazardous heights, and with an envious sigh we'd return to our little poles until grannies and mothers called us all in for the night.

On winter days the best slides were on the pavement of the high road. Somehow the ice was more slippery there, and, of course, the slope steep enough to satisfy the most speed-crazed heart. Arms outstretched to balance us, we'd skim along the silvery surface, cheeks and eyes glowing with joy, feeling we were almost flying. Our feet polished this strip of pavement to lethal slipperiness as far as the adults were concerned, and many a 'currant bun', which was our name for a crash, was suffered by the men next morning on their way to work, or the women with their shopping bags. I can't recall that any bones were broken, but I can remember the roars of fury: 'These weans and their damt slides – I'll belt the next yin I catch making slides on the pavement.' I could never understand their resentment. Surely they knew the pavement had just the right smoothness for slides, and anyway we wouldn't have minded them having a wee shot on our slide even though they hadn't helped to make it.

Sometimes, after our hilarious exercise on the slides, we'd make our way to the 'park', as we called the piece of waste ground behind the houses. We'd clamber up the 'mountains' to our rendezvous at the top, where somebody had run on ahead to start the fire. We were pretending we were gypsies, so we pitched our voices to a low whisper, in case the law was after us. 'Hiv ye brought yer totties?' a hoarse voice demanded. Silently we'd produce one or two potatoes, as many as we could sneak from the shopping, and lay them on the hot glowing embers. As we sat solemnly round in a ring, gazing into the bright heart of the fire while the totties roasted, our eyes were wide and frightened. We dared not look at the darkness pressing at our backs. Oh, but how delicious it was to cup the burning potatoes in cold fingers, and stab with our sharp teeth the blackened curling skin to reach the soft, steaming flesh inside.

When we couldn't get potatoes we occasionally had an orgy with cinnamon stick. This had the very aroma of the sweet spices of the East, although I didn't really like it very much. But it felt so wicked to be sitting in the dark, round a fire, actually smoking this scented tube, that I fully expected the heavens to fall upon me for my wanton ways. I'd been very thoroughly warned, both at home by Grannie and at Sunday School by my teachers, of the penalties of sin. To my amazement, the first time I indulged my baser instincts in this way the heavens stayed just where they were, quite indifferent to my evil behaviour. The absence of heavenly vengeance amazed me, and I wondered if maybe the angels were having a night off themselves.

Another fierce joy was to fill an old pierced tin with rags, set the rags ablaze, and run with this fiery torch into the 'forest', to help my master, Robin Hood. The smouldering rags gave off a fearful stench which clung to everything I wore, but which I didn't even notice, for I was far too busy robbing the rich and helping the poor. I was genuinely amazed when Grannie guessed the minute I came into the house exactly what I'd been up to. 'My heavens,' she'd exclaim, recoiling and seizing her nose, 'your claes are stinking! It's been thae burnt cloots again, you varmint. Into the sink wi' every one o' them. You're no' gaen into ma clean bed wi' a sark smellin' like an auld boot.'

She was deaf to the romance of Robin Hood and I was scrubbed into a state of scarlet cleanliness.

As she picked up the offending clothes she'd stripped off me, Grannie would sigh: 'My goad, we'll never get that smell oot. Ah doot if even the Candy Rock man wid tak' them.'

The Candy Rock man! How we loved him. We'd be in the midst of a game of peever, or ball-beds, or high-speewigh (our name for hide-and-seek), when some courier from another gang would come up panting, 'The Candy Rock man is in Bedlay Street.' Games were abandoned, with never a care as to who was 'het' or who was winning, and we'd stream towards the magic address with one thought in our minds – 'Candy Rock'. When we got there the barrow would be surrounded with wide-eyed children licking eager lips, ready to answer the chant rendered in a high falsetto by our benefactor: 'Who likes Candy Rock, Candy Rock, Candy Rock? Who likes Candy Rock?' Lungs bursting, we would answer with the long-drawn-out 'Me-e-e-e-e-e-e-e' which he liked, and then there would be a waving sea of arms and legs as we scrambled for the thin strips of pink and white rock he scattered amongst us. One school of thought inclined to the view that by shouting 'Not me' they'd establish their characters as unselfish, and that this noble state would be rewarded by all the rock being scattered in their direction. But the other sweets-starved children, of whom I was one, couldn't believe he would think all that out, and we just *knew* he would scatter it in the direction of the loudest and most enthusiastic 'Me-e-e-e'. What fun it was, and what boasting there was afterwards as we compared notes on how many pieces we'd managed to grab and swallow in the short time the sport lasted. It was years, it seemed, before I realized that we were supposed to bring rags in exchange for this lovely striped rock. I had thought it an act of simple generosity, sent to us by the same mysterious Providence who had invented Father Christmas.

But we couldn't rely on getting our sweeties for

nothing very often, for the Candy Rock man's visits weren't nearly frequent enough for our liking, and many a happy hour was spent gazing into the window of Mrs Frame's wee shop, spending our imaginary money. The variety, the colour and selection of good things in those jars and boxes held us spellbound as we squashed our noses against the cold glass. There would be a sharp rat-tat from the inside of the shop, for Mrs Frame wouldn't stand for the steaming up of her spotless plate-glass window, so, reluctantly we'd draw back a little, and resume our discussion as to what we would buy if we had a ha'penny. Seriously we would scan the glittering jars with the boilings and the chocolates at the back of the window, then rake down to the front where sugar mice and dolly mixtures mingled with jelly babies and toffee balls, sherbet dabs and sugarally straps.

And when the time came for me to spend my ha'penny, given to me by Grannie as a reward for some task well done, such as cleaning shoes or drying dishes or sweeping the lobby, I never dreamt of spending all of it on one thing. My plans had been laid, and I sped down to Mrs Frame's on winged feet. 'A faurden's worth o' chewing nuts and a faurden sugarally strap,' I panted. The chewing nuts weren't nuts at all, which seemed perfectly logical to my childish mind, where everything masqueraded as something else and all was make-believe, and these 'nuts' were really tiny pale brown toffees, soft on the outside, with a delicious hard button of a centre, dusted gloriously with sugar and quite, quite irresistible to my palate. For a farthing I got three or four, screwed into a twist of paper, and they lasted me all the way to the grocer's where I was bent on earning my next ha'penny if I was lucky.

The sugarally strap at a farthing hadn't quite the rich quality of a ha'penny nailrod, but that was only just, for it was but half the price. Truly the nailrod was worth a ha'penny, for this piece of liquorice, with its four square sides, like a toothsome pencil, gave a lovely satisfying chew. It was thicker and firmer than the strap, but not so hard as the real liquorice. Still, for a farthing the sugarally strap was quite good value and made most satisfactory make-believe tobacco spit, which was always great fun, even if it outraged Grannie when she heard of it.

Speaking of tobacco, Wee Jeanie's, farther down the road, sold a specially luscious caramel at four a penny, and when the rare mood of luxury was upon me I would toddle into her shop with my farthing, ask for my single caramel, then politely request that she halve it with the tobacco knife so that I could make two bites of it. This knife, which was really intended to cut the men's thick black tobacco into ounce plugs, and half-ounce pieces, was a fascination in itself. I'd watch, spellbound, as Jeanie laid my toffee on the stained board, then brought it forward on its hinge in one swift stroke to smite the sweet exactly in half. My mother used to make a face when told of this transaction, and seemed to think there was something off-putting in mixing the flavours of tobacco and toffee, but if any tobacco was absorbed with the caramel I, in my blissful chewing, never noticed it.

What a choice of goods we had for our farthing! There were tiny sugarally pipes, with little scarlet dots inside the bowl, pretending they were burning tobacco. There were sweetie cigarettes at five for a penny, so naturally a farthing bought one, although it was a bitter disappointment to me that Jeanie wouldn't break the odd one into bits to give me exact justice for my farthing. I wasn't really convinced when she told me, 'Ye aye loss a wee bit, hen, when ye don't buy in bulk,' and I dreamed of the day when I would spend a whole penny and buy *five* cigarettes at once, ration myself carefully over a few days, and gain an extra sweet smoke.

Sweeties had been very expensive after war No 1, and tumbling prices came along in the nick of time for me to enjoy them. Never will I forget the day when the number of aniseed balls went up to forty a penny. There were queues at the wee shop that day, and it was indeed a land of plenty to be given ten balls, hard as iron, for a farthing. I nearly sucked my tongue raw until, with dawning disbelief, I realized I'd have to leave some over for next day. For sweeties to last more than a few minutes was outside my experience until that moment, and it was a marvellous feeling to tuck that wee poke with the three remaining aniseed balls behind Grannie's hankies in the bottom of the chest of drawers, where my brothers couldn't make a raid without either Grannie or me spotting them.

My purchases were always made with farthings and ha'pennies, with maybe a penny when I was going to the Saturday matinée, but beyond those sums I never ventured to think. I never thought of my precious 'savings' as spending money. I put them away and they were as safe as if they were in the Bank of England. But one dizzy day when we were playing 'guesses' in front of Mrs Frame's window a drunk neighbour came up and surveyed us solemnly, blinking as he swayed, listening to our excited 'guesses' and stumbling in exasperation as we rushed past him across to the edge of the pavement when we had made our guess. The edge of the pavement was the finishing line for the winner. When we played guesses with shop goods like this we gave the initial letters of an article in the window, say JB for jelly babies, or WCB for whipped cream bon-bons, and the first to yell out the correct answer leaped for the pavement edge to win. A flight of fancy now made me give PARTW as mine, and when nobody guessed it, my triumphant yells of 'Putty all round the windows' brought a glimmer to the drunk man's face.

He fumbled in his pocket and brought out a handful of coppers. We stood silent, watching him. We were forbidden to talk to strangers, and certainly to drunk men, but we knew this one, alas, for he was a fairly new neighbour. 'Here's a ha'penny for each o' you,' he said ponderously. 'And you, the wee lassie that made the putty guess, here's tuppence for you.' *Tuppence!* For nothing! It was a miracle. It was a fortune.

As I looked at the two coppers, a daring thought sent my head spinning and twisted my stomach with excitement. This money had come for nothing. I hadn't earned it, so I needn't spend it carefully. It was riches galore. I determined to enjoy the thrill of real spending. I drew a deep breath. 'Can I spend it a' on one thing, mister?' I asked. 'On whit?' he said, puzzled. 'On one thing,' I repeated patiently. 'Instead of a faurden's worth of this and a ha'penny worth of that.'

'Spend it ony wey ye like,' he replied grandly as he turned unsteadily towards his house. 'Enjoy yersel', hen, ha'e a real burst.'

I turned to the window and examined every single thing slowly and deliberately. It must be something really wickedly extravagant. Something which wouldn't last, a luxury that would have to be eaten all at once if its flavour and filling were to be fully enjoyed. Suddenly I saw what I wanted.

The others had spent their ha'pennies by the time I went inside the shop, and were chewing happily, waiting for me. There was an awed silence as I demanded imperiously, 'A whipped cream walnut, please.' Mrs Frame smiled and turned to the box. A burst of excited whispering broke out from my chums. 'She's spendin' her hale tuppence on *one* thing.' 'Fancy buying a walnut, and it's that *wee*.' Don't buy it, Molly,' urged one chum. 'It'll a' burst when you bite it, an' ye'll no' be able to keep any till the morn.'

I smiled, deaf to reason, and my teeth fell exultantly on my whole tuppence-worth. It was a glorious moment. I enjoyed every extravagant bite, and I included that drunk man in my prayers for quite a while afterwards.

Three

Even in our asphalt jungle, summer was very notice-able. Windows would be thrown up and left that way all day, instead of being closed tightly against damp and cold. Fires were kept just high enough to do the cook-ing, and the long days seemed always to be warm and golden. This was the time for our running games and our singing games. These songs were surely handed down from generation to generation, and we acted and chanted them, following a ritual which came from we didn't know where. But every movement and gesture was as exact as though it had been choreographed. It seemed as though we had always known words, tune and movement, and I only remember consciously learn-ing one song during my entire childhood. This was 'Ah loast ma hurl on the barra'. It was after Sunday School when I learned it. The big boy and girl who lived in the next close took me home with them to get a taste of their mother's baking of pancakes. As we waited for the hot pancakes to be lifted off the girdle and spread with margarine, the boy started singing, 'Oh the bonnie wee barra's mine', and my ears pricked with interest. For ages I'd sung, 'The barra broke at ten o'clock an' ah loast ma hurl on the barra', and I thought that was the entire song. Now it seemed there was more. 'Sing it again, Henry,' I begged him with great excitement. 'Oh sing it again, I want to know the rest of it.' And by the time we'd finished our pancakes we were all three lustily singing:

> The barra broke at ten o'clock
> An' ah loast ma hurl on the barra.
> Aw the bonnie wee barra's mine,
> It disnae belang tae O'Hara,
> The fly wee bloke, stuck tae ma rock,
> But ah'm gonny stick tae his barra.

I remember teaching a wee English boy, who was on a summer visit to his grannie, to sing:

> Missus MacLean had a wee wean
> She didnae know how to *nurse* it,
> She gi'ed it tae me, an' ah gi'ed it some tea,
> An' its wee belly *burstit*.

I was enchanted to hear this old Glasgow song rendered with a prissy English accent, and kept making him sing it for me. I was astounded one day when he refused. 'But why?' I asked him, 'I thought you liked that wee song.' 'My grannie says I'm not to sing it any more,' he said primly. 'She says it's vulgar.' Vulgar! I'd never heard the word before, and didn't know what it meant. When I asked my grannie, she laughed and said,

'Och well, you ken whit the English are like. Butter widnae melt in their mooths, to hear them. The word
"belly" will likely be too coorse for them.' Belly too
coorse! But it was in the Bible, and we called our navels
our belly buttons without shame or thought. I wondered what else I said that was vulgar. I'd have to be
careful. Maybe I was constantly being vulgar without
knowing it. Grannie dismissed my fears, and said there
was nothing wrong with the wee harmless songs we
sang, and I was to go out and play and not to be so daft.

So we saw nothing to cause a raised eyebrow when
we chanted as we ran through the closes:

> A hundred and ninety-nine,
> Ma faither fell in the bine,
> Ma mother came oot wi' the washin' cloot,
> An' skelped his bare behind!

One which caused us great hilarity because of the
cheeky wee soldier's behaviour in church was:

> Ma wee laud's a sojer,
> He comes fae Maryhull,
> He gets his pey on Friday night,
> An' buys a hauf-a-jull.
> He goes tae church on Sundays,
> A hauf an 'oor late.
> He pulls the buttons aff his shirt,
> An' pits them in the plate!

And there was one we used to act, just showing our heads out of the staircase window, as though we weren't properly dressed and daren't lean out farther:

Ah'm no' comin' oot the noo, the noo,
Ah'm no' comin' oot the noo.
Ah'm very sorry Lizzie MacKay, for disappointin' you.
Ma mother's away wi' ma claes tae the pawn
To raise a bob or two.
An' ah've juist a fur aroon' ma neck,
So ah'm no' comin' oot the noo.

In our songs it was the wives who left the husbands, for there was something funny in a man being left to look after the house.

There was a lilting one which went:

Ma wife ran awa' an' left me,
Left me a' ma lane.
Ah'm a simple chap.
Ah widnae care a rap,
If she hadnae run awa' an' left the wean.

And a slower chant, which we sang in a slurred tone as if we'd had a wee bit too much to drink:

Wa's comin' wi' me?
Ah'm oot on the spree.
Ma wife's awa' on the train,

44

Ah hope ah niver see her again.
Ah'm havin' the time of my life,
Plenty of L.S.D.,
I'm off the teetotal,
I've ta'en tae the bottle.
So wha's comin' wi' me?

And a nice one for singing with a sob in the throat was:

Ah've got the dishes tae wash,
An' the flairs tae scrub.
Nicht an' day ah'm niver away
Fae the washin' tub.
She does whitever she likes,
An' ah dae the best ah can.
Jimmy McPhee can easily see
Ah'm a mere, mere, man.

These were the Glasgow back-court songs which we added to our repertoire of the games played all over the country at their appropriate season. 'Queen Mary, Queen Mary my age is sixteen', 'Broken bridges falling down', 'The Bonnie bunch o' Roses', 'Down in yonder valley where the green grass grows', and 'Water water wallflower, growing up so high'. We moved delicately through the movements, oblivious of mothers and grannies who occasionally glanced our way from their tenement windows, self-absorbed and transported into a graceful mannered world.

We were merciless on those who couldn't or wouldn't learn the movements fast enough, and who spoilt the rhythm, and we'd pounce on the hapless novice and put her through it again and again until she got fed up. She'd stalk away from us and walk to the middle of the back court and address herself to an upper window, 'Mammy, throw us ower a piece.' We pretended to ignore her and our own dawning hunger, and she went on repeating her monotonous chant till a window was thrown up, a head appeared briefly, disappeared, and then a paper bag sailed earthwards, to land on the baked clay of the back court with a most satisfying smack. It was a lovely sound to our ears. A sound which meant cut fresh bread spread with margarine or, in odd moments of affluence, butter, or, favourite choice of the entire back-court children, a delicious layer of home-made raspberry or strawberry jam.

When the hungry one returned to the group the sight of her drooling jaws sent several more strolling to the centre of the back court to take up the cry, and before long only the most dedicated girls were acting out their fantasies in the singing games – the others had abandoned themselves to the enjoyment of their jeely pieces.

I don't know what other mothers thought of this behaviour, but my grannie felt it was extremely vulgar (we both knew the word now, and it could be applied to many things). She sternly forbade me to indulge in it. Only if I could plead that I was actually starving, say on my return from the swimming baths, did I dare find courage to raise my voice and give vent to the familiar cry.

Up would go the window, and Grannie's outraged face would appear between sill and sash. 'Wheest, you limmer, haud yer tongue. If you want a piece you'll have to come up an' get it.' And the window was slammed down. This was real strategy on her part, for she knew I'd have to be really hungry to climb four flights of stairs and face her irritation at being stopped in the middle of her housework. And nothing short of real hunger would let her encourage me to nibble between meals and put me off the real food she was preparing for my growth and enjoyment.

Usually her ruse worked, and I'd turn despondently away, kicking the stones and pretending I didn't care, while the others jeered at me, their mouths stuffed with bread.

Sometimes, however, when she was in an indulgent mood, Grannie would spread two pieces of thin white bread with fresh margarine or, if we were having an extravagant week with my mother's overtime money, a thin scraping of fresh butter, which was as rare as caviare on our budget, wrap it in a white paper bag and send it plummeting towards me. The thrill of sharing the 'piece' with the other children invested the food with a sort of magic, and never did bread eaten at a prosaic table taste so satisfying or delicious. Like the 'chittering bite' eaten at the baths, the back-court piece had a flavour all its own, which was never recaptured elsewhere.

The height of luxury was reached when on rare occasions we were given two tea biscuits pressed together, with fresh butter squeezing through the tiny holes, making a most agreeable pattern. It was no trouble to climb the stairs for this treat, for if they broke in their flight from window to back court the artistic effect of the smooth disc of buttery points was lost, and I enjoyed looking at it nearly as much as eating it.

Once, in a flight of exotic fancy, somebody put half a bar of cream chocolate between the bread and butter, and we watched her with awe as she bit through this splendid mixture. I tried it myself at the very first opportunity, i.e., when I could bring myself to use fourpence from my savings as a birthday treat, and I shivered with delight at my extravagance rather than with pleasure at the flavour.

In the same field of gourmet experiment was 'a piece on chips'. Dieticians would have shuddered at all this starch, but to our palates there was something at once filling and exciting about the flavour of the deep fried potatoes which melted the butter as they were pressed between the slices of buttered bread.

Another great treat was 'a piece on condensed milk'. Sickly, sweet, but different in the most acceptable sense of the word. And, of course, 'a piece on sugar' or 'sugar and oatmeal' was delicious, although some spoil-sports warned us that it would give us all worms! I never knew anybody who had worms, although I'd often seen worm-cakes in the chemist, and a spice of danger was added to enjoyment as we dipped buttered pieces into wee paper pokes of mixed meal and sugar.

'A piece on black treacle' was a rare delight, but this had to be eaten quickly, before the treacle seeped into the bread and turned it a horrible fawn colour which ruined enjoyment. Golden syrup made a lovely piece, and caraway seeds a strange one which I tried hard to like because Grannie ate hers with such obvious relish.

We never aspired to a sandwich in the true sense. We never dreamt of meat, or cheese, or eggs, or fish. They were real meals, to be eaten at dinner-time or tea-time, and not lightly to be consumed for fun. No, for between meals it had to be sweet and simple spreads, and all that sugar and treacle and syrup seemed to give us boundless energy for the dozens of thrilling, absorbing games which filled the endless leisure hours.

The Cooperative Store was the hub of our shopping activities. How else could working-class people shop on credit, and earn a little dividend at the same time? It always seemed to be packed with customers. In all the years I ran the messages for Grannie I never remember the shop being empty. Along one side ran the long mahogany counter with female clerks perched on high stools, whose job it was to write down our orders in our 'store' books. Along the opposite side ran the long wooden counter attended by the serving grocers, usually male. In the territory in between there was constant movement as customers moved over to be served, where boys barged back and forth with huge baskets balanced on their heads, filled with 'delivery orders', and men staggered in under heavy loads of steaming bread, and where customers finally tottered out with their filled shopping baskets.

When you arrived at the shop you dropped your 'book' in the slotted box at the end of the mahogany counter, and a quick glance showed if there would be time for a game of peever or ball-beds on the pavement outside before your name would be called. This risk had to be weighed very carefully, for if you missed your turn your book went to the end of the queue again. Ball-beds were a special temptation, as well as a time hazard, for the 'beds' had to be drawn on the pavement with chalk, the names of the players put in little artistically scalloped compartments at the top end of the beds, and then we took turns to bounce our ball in an intricate pattern from one bed to another according to the numbered squares, without touching a single line with either feet or ball. You could only chance this delightful time-consuming game if there was a huge stack of books in the box ahead of you. So sometimes it was safer to stay inside the shop and play at 'guesses', and as our Co-op only changed its display about once a month, the children playing 'guesses' knew the stock better than the grocer. It was well-nigh impossible to surprise an opponent with a new item, so you were reduced to tricks like 'SOTF' which meant 'sawdust on the floor' – technically this wasn't allowed, but such infringements of the rules were a great test of ingenuity, and the variations endless.

The grown-ups drove us to a frenzy with their endless chatter with the female clerks as they gave orders. There was an atmosphere in the Co-op unlike any other shop. With books having names and addresses clearly displayed, everyone was known by name, and it seemed to us that getting the messages entered in books and ledgers was the last thought in the minds of women on both sides of the counter. While we fidgeted, not daring to leave because it was getting near our turn, details would be exchanged of the latest wedding, or funeral, or Mrs So-an-So's operation, or the latest baby, etc., etc. We suffered in silence, for the slightest bit of cheek soon brought a clout on the ear from an outraged adult. All mothers were united in their treatment of impudent kids, and a skelp from a stranger was no novelty in our world. Wild as we were in many ways, we had to keep our place in the presence of grown-ups, and nobody thought we would come to any harm by repressing our impatience.

The only thing that made the gossiping women move, tut-tutting with annoyance, was when it drew near lunchtime or evening closing time, and the ritual of the sawdust-sweeping began. We children loved it, of course, if only as a diversion. Out from the back shop appeared the boy, importantly swinging a bottle full of water with a pierced cork stopper, and how we admired and envied him as he swung it expertly, scattering the clean shower over the sawdust floor. It was one of my fiercest ambitions to be allowed to wield that bottle, and watch the women jump as the splashes hit their solid legs. When I first saw this operation I imagined it was vinegar the boy was using, for my only other experience of a pierced cork stopper was in the fish-and-chip shop, but even the later discovery that it was only water didn't put me off.

Having laid the dust expertly, the boy then briskly swept up all the dirty sawdust, using a long-handled stiff broom, and customers who'd escaped the water leaped out of his way as his sweeps grew longer and wider. When all was clean, he reappeared with a square biscuit tin filled with clean sawdust which he deftly scattered over the entire floor. It was as good as a circus, and in our eyes he was the star turn.

When I first started shopping for Grannie I was so wee that I had to stand on my basket to see over the counter to make sure I wasn't being given short weight, hard bacon or outside loaves. As I grew a few inches, the basket turned over on its side was high enough, and then at long last the glorious day arrived, after a holiday at the seaside, when I found I could stand with my feet in the sawdust and rest my chin on the counter and see absolutely everything without any help at all. It was at the Co-op that I learned to accept teasing about my height and my name. 'Weir,' the assistant called out as my turn came to be served. Then, holding up two black puddings and winking all round, he would say, 'This is a wee-er black pudding than that one, so I think your grannie would like it better.' The laughter was good-natured and I enjoyed the joke too.

I loved seeing the new bread being delivered. It arrived in long rows, and as each two-pound loaf was sold, it was separated from its neighbours in most satisfactory clouds of steam.

In the back shop, potatoes were housed in a huge bunker which had a little sliding door in the front, near the bottom, just large enough for the 'tottie-boy' to push in his shovel and rattle down the necessary amount, which he'd toss on to a large scale standing beside the bunker. This was another enviable task performed by the sawdust boy. He seldom had to alter the weights, for nearly everybody in our tenements bought a quarter of a stone. If his sharp shovel was careless it would cut into a potato and savagely cut and blacken it, causing Grannie to tut-tut angrily if my watchful eye had missed it. I always enjoyed my glimpses of the back shop, for the bunker and the big shovel, the all-enveloping heavy apron worn by the boy, and the earthiness of the potatoes combined to create an atmosphere very different from the dull ordinariness of the rest of the shop.

Eggs were very precious when I was a wee girl. They were so scarce and so expensive that no grocer would guarantee to replace a bad egg without evidence that the egg hadn't been eaten. Like doubting Thomas, he had to *see* the offending egg, which often stank to high heaven. Many of the older women would reel back, holding their noses, and call appealingly to the grocer, 'For goodness' sake, Jimmy, let the wean take that egg roon' the back afore her turn, or ah'll be seeck!'

The rotten eggs had to be taken round to the midden in the backyard next to the shop, where a boy was stationed to make sure the eggs actually went into the foul-smelling bins. This was to ensure no unscrupulous person would offer the same egg twice. It was my delight to volunteer to take the rotten eggs of the older women to this reeking depository, an offer which was thankfully accepted, and I enjoyed tossing the egg with unerring aim straight into the centre of the bin. No wonder I was so good at coconut shies when 'the shows' came round to our district – I'd had regular practice with rotten eggs.

Syrup and treacle, which we loved, weren't always easy to get, and I remember one day when we were all playing with our marbles on the pavement the cart arrived piled high with jams and jellies in their unmistakable boxes, and, at the side, two huge chests marked 'Syrup' and 'Treacle'. There was a wild scatter as we each reclaimed our store of 'bools' before we rushed home for the store books and the netbags, then out again to form a noisy, chattering queue. After at least a two-hour vigil, for the cart had to be unloaded and checked first, we had our reward. Black treacle was a passion with me at that time and I'd cheerfully have stood all day if at the end of it I could have had a piece on treacle. Well, this particular consignment had been delivered in cartons – not tins – and I laid mine carefully into my netbag. Alas, in my ignorance of the weakness of the new container, I put it at the bottom of the bag, upside down. And the tragedy was revealed only when I felt something warm and sticky running down my ankles.

The skelp I got from Grannie when she saw the mess and realized the waste, wasn't entirely responsible for my tears.

Everything that was bought at the Co-op was marked in the book, and no money changed hands until pay-day, when maybe a pound would be paid in towards the week's shopping, and the mothers usually attended to this payment themselves instead of leaving it to the children. On one bitter occasion, when I was entrusted with a pound, I put it into my coat pocket and stood quietly in the shop, not daring to go outside to play in case I'd lose it. And then, while I was waiting, I got so carried away with the new stock which had arrived, and with my stupendous success at 'guesses', that I didn't notice a thieving hand quietly rob me of the precious note. Only when I came to pay was the loss discovered, and we all searched the sawdust till our eyes and noses stung with the particles and the dust. But I knew with sickening certainty that we wouldn't find it. I knew I had been robbed. It was a terrible moment having to tell my mother, for she had just lost her job and had only ten shillings in the world after giving me that pound. It says much for her understanding that, in spite of her thin purse, one look at my stricken face told her I needed no other punishment. Tenement children didn't have to be told the value of money, we knew it only too well.

Two doors down from the grocery section of the Co-op was the drapery department, which also sold shoes. My grannie bought a pair of shoes every summer, before we went on our holidays, and I felt very important when I was sent down to bring back several pairs 'on appro' so that she could try them on in the privacy of her own home. I never really knew what 'on appro' meant. I only knew they were magic words which, once uttered, entitled me to obtain three or four splendid cardboard boxes containing spanking new shoes, and that nothing was marked 'in the book' until we had made our decision. The excitement of trying to persuade Grannie to have the ones with the buckles, which she instantly dismissed as far too frivolous, and the responsibility of taking back the ones she didn't want, and then, and only then, having the price marked in the book, had me fairly bursting with importance and a sense of occasion.

When it was our turn to have shoes bought for us, shoes which we wore only on Sundays, we were taken to the central branch, at the other end of Springburn, where there was a bigger selection. How proud we felt as we sat on squeaking chairs, only to be whisked out of them the moment an adult was seen to be standing.

My mother stood no nonsense, but we didn't mind. Sitting or standing, we entered into the full drama of each stranger's purchase with as keen an interest as though the shoes were for our own feet. We criticized the quality, the colour, the price, the suitability of the shoe for its purpose. Nobody felt rushed, for we all knew that shoes had to last for a very long time, and money was scarce and we couldn't afford to make a mistake. When our turn came we tried to kick our battered and scuffed old boots under the chair out of sight. How shaming they seemed compared with the splendid new leather which now stiffly encased our feet. But their scuffed comfort lent wings to our feet as we ran home with our new shoe-box, and climbed on to a chair to lay the new shoes reverently on top of the wardrobe, out of harm's way until we drew them on on Sunday when we went to church.

There was a Co-op about every five hundred yards in our district, but you got to know your own Co-op as though it were a club, and how alien other Co-ops seemed if you were sent there by a neighbour. But your own! Ah, that was different. So cosy. So chummy. The girl clerks in our Co-op lent me a new pen nib, shiny and smooth, for each school examination, and later for those I sat at college, and they rejoiced in my successes all the more because they had supplied the nibs which had written the answers.

They actually encouraged me to act my little stories as I waited my turn. This was amazing to me, for

Grannie discouraged 'showing off' and described me as 'a Jezebel' if I dared imitate anything I had seen on the screen at Saturday matinées. And I found the packed Co-op a marvellous source of fun when I'd play practical jokes, the favourite being covering myself with sparkling frost and running in, panting, as though for shelter, pretending it was pelting with rain. This was especially mystifying when the sun was shining, but in our temperamental climate the trick worked every time, to my joy.

But for certain items my mother had her favourite shops, and I felt positively breathless with patronage as I went into those little specialized establishments. The one nearest our home was owned by a father and two daughters. The father was dark and saturnine, and the daughters placid, plump and fair. The father looked permanently in a seething temper. He probably had a bad stomach, but we took him as we found him and decided he was just naturally bad-tempered. 'Mean as get out,' my mother assured us. 'He'd take a currant off the scale to make sure you didn't get a skin over weight.' But his home-cooked boiled beef ham was her passion, and his spiced pork delicious. I was fascinated to watch him shake the spice from a canister with a pierced lid, and my mouth watered as I raced home, hardly able to wait to get my tiny portion spread on bread and margarine, and savour this aromatic food. I always liked it when the daughter with her hair done up in earphones served me. She was dreamy and far-away and quite capable of ignoring her father's sharp glance as the scale wavered past the quarter-pound to give me an extra half-slice with my order. Oh that was bliss indeed! The other daughter, though, hair in a bun on top of her head, was her father's own child. Exact weight and no more, and I avoided her when I could, and gazed intently at the coloured boxes on the shelves until the earphoned goddess was free.

For home-cooked gammon we went to the little cooked meats shop at the top of the hill. It was always a pleasure to watch the owner-cum-cook slice the perfectly boiled gammon with his thin, viciously sharp knife, and lay it reverently, slice by mouth-watering slice, on the fine grease-proof paper, and then transfer the savoury load to the marble scale. This was a splendid character, rosy-cheeked, with a mop of wiry, curly black hair, a man who obviously enjoyed his work. Sometimes, to my joy, he passed over a sliver of the gammon on his knife, to let me drool over its flavour while he cut the quarter I'd ordered. Not every time, for this would have been spoiling indeed, but often enough to make an errand to his shop have all the excitement of a lucky dip.

We knew every mannerism of each assistant to the last nose-twitch. We had plenty of time to observe them, warts and all, in those busy shops in pre-refrigerator days, when shopping had to be done every day. One of my favourites was the man behind the cheese counter in a big store, privately owned of course, in the centre of Glasgow. He clearly loved his work. He reigned over the cheeses like a captain over his ship. He stood, white-aproned, behind his counter, and surveyed us all calmly, a brooding responsibility keeping his face very serious. Behind him, a vast range of swelling rounds of cheeses were arrayed. On the marble ledge in front of him smaller cuts rested, with wire-cutters neatly to hand. Each transaction was a little ritual. No plastic-wrapped portions for this expert. A gentleman in a trilby, inquiring about the merits of a particular cheese, would have a tiny portion removed by the wire-cutters and handed to him to savour. The cheese salesman would stand back, mouth pursed, eyes watchful, as the customer slowly chewed the morsel, while the rest of us awaited the result with keenest interest. We weren't impatient. This thoughtful consideration seemed absolutely right to us. At last the trilby-hatted gentleman would nod, 'Mmmm. Yes. Excellent. I'll take a pound, please.' A sigh from the cheese-man and from us, the audience. 'I thought you would like it, sir. A very mature cheese, and excellent with a drop of port.' Port! This was high living with a vengeance, and the humble purchaser of two ounces of Cheddar felt for a moment exalted to undreamt-of realms of luxury.

This cheese salesman was a wizard with the wire-cutters, and could cut a huge virgin cheese with the speed and accuracy of a circular saw, and extract an exact two ounces or four ounces to a milligram. He would have been chagrined beyond words to have to add the words: 'An extra ha'penny, or a penny under or over.' You asked for four ounces and you got four ounces. He was admired by all of us, for we knew an artist when we saw one.

Another exclusive grocer's in town was an Aladdin's cave to me. I loved going there with a chum who collected a weekly box of special biscuits for the minister. There was a little stone bowl at the door, filled with clean drinking water so that customers' dogs might be refreshed. The mahogany and plate-glass doors had the weight and opulence of a bank entrance, and the well-polished counters were ranged with strange, exotic foods. Things I'd never heard of, much less eaten. Truffles. Foie gras. Peaches in brandy. Calves-foot jelly. This last particularly fascinated me, and I couldn't for the life of me decide when this should be eaten. 'It's invalid food,' somebody assured me when I whispered my puzzlement over this delicacy. But what was an invalid? I'd never heard this grand name used to describe somebody in poor health, and I continued to puzzle whether or not the invalid would spread the jelly on bread, as we did with my mother's home-made black currant, or whether she would sup it with her dinner; calf sounded like meat to me.

But I had no doubt whatever that the owner and his son were the two luckiest men in the world to be able to preside over this wonderland every working day of their lives. Fancy dealing with scented China tea, chicken in aspic, curries, spices, and even stem ginger!

Father and son were immaculate in their dress, as befitted the stock they handled. Dark suits, sparkling white shirts, perfect bow ties and gleaming shirt-cuffs. The food was parcelled in thick, expensive, crackling brown paper and fine strong string, and the son had a fascinating mannerism of shrugging his shoulders in sharp little movements as he deftly stroked down the corners of the paper to form a perfect seal to the package. I watched him with unwinking gaze, admiring every movement of those expressive shoulders, and envied him nearly as much as I did the Principal Boy in the pantomime, for it seemed to me they both lived in magic worlds.

And in our own much humbler district the shop we all loved best was owned by a somewhat frightening spinster lady always known as 'Miss P.' Nobody, not even the most chatty grown-up, ever called her by her Christian name, and nobody had ever seen her without a hat. She always dressed in black. Black silk blouse, held at the neck by a gold and Cairngorm brooch. Black, highly polished shoes and black lisle stockings. Surmounting a head of rusty auburn hair, she wore a black felt hat in winter and a black straw in summer. She had rosy cheeks and fierce black eyes, and knew her stock to the last shoelace. I liked her shop best of all in summer, with its rows and rows of sand-shoes hanging temptingly at the door-front, fastened to a long line of strong twine from top to bottom of the door-hinges. I would stand mesmerized in front of them. White ones wooed my heart, but, of course, they'd never have kept clean enough to be practical. Navy ones would match my gym slip. Black ones looked exciting and grown-up, but the grey ones, with little speckles of black, looked most elegant and were my favourites. Oh the excitement when my mother would take us in on a chosen Saturday, to rig us out with our sand-shoes for summer holidays, and for running about at our games during the long long days of summer, to save our heavier more expensive boots and Sunday shoes. Although our sand-shoes cost only about two-and-eleven a pair, Miss P. treated us with the courtesy due to honoured clients. We were seated on brightly polished chairs, our noses filled with the delicious scent of the rubber soles carried to us by the breeze from the shoes by the door. She consulted my mother as to colour and size, then with unerring eye she would cut off a pair of shoes from the rows hanging at the door. The very stuff of summer holidays was in the sensation felt as those soft shoes encased the feet, so different from the rigid leather of the long-legged boots which were my workaday school-day wear, or the formal splendour of my black patent lacing shoes for Sundays. A pair of new shoelaces would be threaded through, and I would stand before the little floor mirror, ready to leap into the air like a shorn lamb, drunk with the feeling of lightness in my feet. The shoelaces cost an extra penny, but sometimes Miss P. was in generous mood, no doubt realizing how precious every penny was to my hardworking mother, and she would present us with the laces free of charge. My mother's eyes would glow as brightly as Miss P.'s, at this generosity, and she would say, as we left with our parcel, 'Aye, a real lady, Miss P. It's a pleasure to be served by her.'

Four

The first thing my mother examined when she was looking at any possible new house was the kitchen range. You could always disguise faulty windows with nice curtains, and put an extra shelf into a press that was too wee or awkward, but you were stuck with a range, and if it didn't 'draw' properly, or had been too neglected, it was a plague and a torment.

So we always made sure we had a good range. It was the centre of warmth and comfort, and the very hub of our busy kitchen. It stood along the dividing wall between us and the next-door neighbour, exactly half-way between the sink and the inset bed, spreading heat and cheer, and enjoyed by all of us from first light till bedtime, for the kitchen was bedroom, cooking place and living-room combined.

Its steely parts were burnished and its black parts black-leaded once a week, and a great ceremony that was. Grannie would spread newspapers out on the floor to protect linoleum and hearth-rug. The long stool which usually held pride of place before the glow-ing coals would be pushed back out of the way, and the Zebo and cleaning cloths spread out in readiness.

All the movable steel parts were lifted aside – the

'winter', as Grannie called the steel piece which formed a small shelf in front of the glowing bars, the ashpan, the front barred section and the oven door.

Then slowly and methodically Grannie would Zebo the stripped monster that remained, making sure every bit of grease disappeared and every piece of cast iron got its black coating. I was never allowed to touch this part of the operation, for, as Grannie scathingly remarked, 'You'd have the hale kitchen covered in black'ning,' but I loved watching her, especially when it came to the polishing off of the Zebo. Huge cloths brought everything up to a gleaming ebony, and then when you felt it just couldn't shine any brighter the final touch was given with a soft polishing brush which reached every crevice, and the range gleamed like dusky satin.

But I *was* allowed to tackle the 'steels', as we called the other parts which had been laid aside. With emery paper and a judicious use of a little 'spit' on small rust spots these were burnished to a silvery glitter, and as I rubbed and panted I was urged on by Grannie to use 'plenty o' elbow grease'. A final polish with a soft duster to remove any lingering dust left by the emery paper, and I glowed nearly as brightly as the steels at Grannie's praise. 'Aye, ye've made a grand job o' them lassie, they're like silver, juist like pure silver.'

The fire, of course, had been allowed to go out so that we could work at the range closely and comfortably, and now, when we had got everything shining and sparkling to Grannie's satisfaction, and the steels back

66

in place, came the ceremony of lighting the fire. Screwed-up newspaper went in first, then the sticks were laid criss-cross to support the coal which was laid on top. Nothing must be packed too tightly or the air wouldn't get through and let it 'draw' – it was a great art, and a terrible disgrace if it didn't burn at first setting and had all to be taken apart, and laid all over again. Soon the flames were dancing and the fire roaring, and reflecting itself a dozen times on the black satin and silver glitter of our polished surfaces.

Once a month there was an additional ritual known fearsomely as 'cleaning the flues'. I didn't exactly know what a 'flue' was, but it obviously had to be treated with great caution and respect. Grannie would wrap her head in newspapers, looking like one of the mammies in *Uncle Tom's Cabin*, then she would take a long iron cleek in one hand, while with the other she would open a little sliding hatch above the empty fire, very very carefully.

A shovel and more paper were laid across the fire to catch any falling soot, and then, like an archaeologist after hidden treasure, Grannie would very gently poke the long cleek into the hidden cavern, exploring all the mysterious corners, to dislodge every lurking particle of soot.

We were in constant terror of the 'jeests', as Grannie called the joists, catching fire, for she assured us as she poked about the flues that if this happened then the whole building would blaze, and the next tenement as well, for those joists ran right up the height of the tenements inside the walls and could set flames roaring from close to top flat.

This was no exaggerated fear, for I remember one terrible night, when I was about four years old, wakening to see the kitchen full of firemen, who, under my dreamy gaze, broke the wall with their axes to get at the 'jeests', which had indeed caught fire in a flat below ours, and the flames roared into our kitchen the moment the wall was breached. While the tallest fireman fought the blaze, I inquired with interest, 'Are you Jack and the beanstalk?', and there was a cry of alarm as I was snatched from the bed, 'My Goad, I forgoat the wean was there.'

When the firemen were trying to trace the source of the fire my grannie enlightened them. 'It'll be thae dirty rascals doon below,' she said grimly. 'I ken fine that besom never touches her flues fae one year's end to the other.'

Every bit of our range was used for cooking. The kettle was always on the side of the hob and only needed moving over the flames at any time to bring it to full boiling point for cups of tea, or pease brose, or anything else we wanted. Beef tea sat simmering at the back of the hob when any of us needed this nourishing brew after illness. The big soup pot stood at the other side, slowly blending the good vegetables into a grand broth which, using a favourite phrase, Grannie declared, would 'stick to your ribs and see you through the winter'. The stew pot wasn't far away, and there was still plenty of room for the pot which held the potatoes.

A small hook at the side worked a grid which let the heat from the fire into the oven and Grannie was expert at knowing just how high the fire ought to be for scones and cakes, and how low it could go so the oven heat would be just right to finish off bread, or the roast at Christmas time.

When the top of the range was covered with pots, and Grannie wanted to make a bit of ham and egg for my mother coming in from work, she would lay strips of ham in a shallow baking tin, carefully break an egg over them, and then prop the tin at just the correct angle in front of the glowing fire to let everything grill gently and evenly. What a delicious smell would waft through the kitchen, and how fascinating we children found this method of cooking, watching with bated breath the tiny bubbles forming as the bacon took the heat of the fire, and the egg slowly firmed but never over-cooked. And, of course, we toasted our bread at the glowing bars, and were warmed through and through at the same time.

In bitter weather, the 'winter', that little steel shelf, was unhooked from the front bars of the fire, and a piece of flannel wrapped round it to protect our toes, and how comforting it was to put our stockinged feet against it as we supped our pease brose or hot gruel before we went to bed. Our grannie found the wee 'winter' a great economy, for it heated itself at no cost at all, just by sitting in its place on the range and taking its warmth from the coals.

The long stool which ran the length of the range, standing on the hearth-rug, became our favourite dining place as children. We sat on the hearth-rug like worshippers before a shrine, gazing into the glowing heart of the flames, and watched with laughter our distorted reflection in the shining steels, while we sipped our tea or cocoa and munched our rolls before going to school or to bed.

The last sound I heard at night before falling asleep was made by the steel door being shut in front of the bars, to make sure no coal fell out during the night. The first sharp sound when I wakened was the ashpan being drawn out, and the ashes tipped into a bucket, ready to be taken down to the 'midden' when I went out for the breakfast rolls. There was a right and a wrong way to empty those ashes. 'Noo, stand close ower the pail, lassie,' Grannie would say, 'and tim it in quietly and slowly, so ye'll no' get the stour a' ower yer claes.'

Each range had its own personality and took a bit of knowing before one understood all its little ways, and I think the hardest thing to part from when we moved house was surely this beloved monster, the kitchen range.

Everything in the tenement kitchens was called into use by the children and used as equipment for games. Among all the kitchen fixtures I think our first favourite was the bunker. It was a plain modest thing of varnished wood with a hinged lid on top. A hinged flap on the front let down when the coal was getting near the bottom, so that we could reach down easily with the shovel and get at the last of 'the churlies', as Grannie called the small coal. To the right of it was the dresser, of the same varnished wood, its two top drawers filled to overflowing with dusters and tea-cloths and cutlery, plus all the paraphernalia of our games – our peeries, our peevers, our football cards, cigarette cards, skipping rope, bools (or marbles) and jawries. Under this dresser was a cupboard, where the pots and pans were stowed, the pipeclay for the stairs, the black-lead for the range, and the Angier's emulsion and Parish's chemical food, two great stand-bys against our winter colds and spring lassitude.

The whole arrangement seemed excellent to us, and we were aghast when we heard of some people who had actually banished the bunker out to the stair landing so that the coalman needn't come into the house with his dirty boots. Fancy removing such a treasure from the warmth of the kitchen, we thought, and we felt sorry for the children of such finicky folk, being deprived of such a splendid plaything. For that was how we saw our bunker. It was *much* more than a mere receptacle for coal. It was our toy. Our play-pen. A permanent source of joy and entertainment and we never wearied of it all the days of our childhood.

On wet days, when we couldn't get out to play, the

bunker was a favourite place to hide when we played hide-and-seek, although my heart was always in my mouth in case my brothers, in a fit of devilment, would fasten the wee sneck and keep me there against my will. But it was such an enchanted darkness that I suffered this fear willingly, for the fun of peeping through the line of daylight at the flap-hinge watching the chums trying to find me. Of course, once inside the bunker, you were stuck there until the searchers ran into the best front room or the lobby, and then what a scramble it was to get over the rocky coal, to clatter open the flap and leap out and race for the 'den' to announce myself uncaught, with another chance of hiding.

During spring-cleaning times my mother would have the fanciful idea of whitewashing the inside of the bunker, although I can't think how she hoped to keep it clean for any length of time, considering it was usually full of black coal. Although Grannie and she cheerfully accepted the stour and dust on our clothes when we played in the bunker, they were both surprisingly furious when we appeared streaked with whitewash as well! I never could understand why the whitewash was worse than the coal dust, but I obligingly dusted myself down to please them.

Another favourite game was to lean a wooden plank against the bunker, climb on to the lid, and slide down this home-made chute, landing with a whoop on the kitchen floor. Our downstairs neighbour was most understanding, and accepted with placid grace the noise that surely must result from the playtime of three lively children when the weather kept them indoors. Mind you, she stood no nonsense when we ran about the house with our heavy boots, which was strictly forbidden by Grannie, and she'd knock the ceiling with her long wooden pole to let us know she was annoyed. When we heard this we'd gaze at one another with stricken eyes and change into our slippers without a word having to be said.

Sometimes the bunker was used by us for more serious things, and its lid became a desk when we spread it with our school books as we wrestled with homework, and pored over our jotters. Occasionally we had to make way for Grannie, so that she could use the top for cooling trays of toffee or pots of jam, and then we'd lean against it with covetous eyes, waiting for the toffee to cool and exasperating Grannie by poking with experimental fingers to see if the toffee was ready for breaking and eating.

About once in four weeks my mother, as she left for work in the morning, would remind Grannie 'Oh, Grannie, don't forget to get the bunker ready – the coal's coming today.' There was a fierce scurry on our part to move our treasures out of harm's way, so that the lid could be raised in readiness for the coalman. 'My drumsticks!' Tommy would cry, and move them carefully to the top of the dresser. 'My scraps!' I'd yell, and take my adored coloured angels and fairies, and lay them safely under the bed as a temporary refuge. 'My bools!' Willie would shout, and slide the saucer with his plunkers and jawries and glessies, the most prized marbles he possessed, to the far end of the dresser. Meantime Grannie took down the brass covers hanging along the back wall so that the lid could go right back unhindered.

Then the first faint cry would reach us, increasing in strength as the coalman mounted the stairs. 'Yeeee-how!', which we correctly translated as 'Coal', followed by 'WEEEEEEEE . . . R', delivered in a long-drawn-out bellow which would have wakened the dead. At last he would stride into our kitchen, a gigantic figure in our eyes. Face blackened with coal dust, lips showing a rim of scarlet behind the black crust which had formed as he licked them, teeth startlingly white and gums gleaming pink as he grinned at us. This visitor in glorious Technicolor fascinated us. We admired the superb strength of him as he tossed the coal into the depths of the empty bunker, and appreciated his thoughtfulness as he smoothed out the bag deftly so that too much dust wouldn't rise to blacken Grannie's spotless shelves.

'How many bags are we gettin' the day, mister?' we would ask. 'Will it be right tae the top?' 'Right tae the top!' he would reply. 'Yer grannie'll hiv tae burn plenty o' fires afore there's room for you to play in the bunker.' He knew as well as we did that the bunker was more than just a thing for coal.

The tenements were all lit by gas, and on Fridays when Grannie and I were doing the cleaning of all the brasses in the house the mantle had to be removed from the thin brass gas bracket with its swan-like neck, and moved to safety, while we set to with busy polish and cloths and made the bracket and the band which ran round the mantelpiece sparkle like beaten gold.

Sometimes when handing the mantle back to Grannie for replacing on the bracket my fingers would grasp it too tightly and I'd hear a screech, 'My goodness, that's anither mantle awa'. Whit'll your mother say? How often have I to tell you that ye canna handle a mantle like a bool? Awa' doon to the store and get anither ane.'

The assistant would cock a quizzical eye as I asked, 'One inverted gas mantle please.' 'Imphm! And who broke it this time, hen? You? Or yer grannie?' 'Me,' I had to confess. As he handed me the little square cardboard box, he'd say, 'Weel, don't run wi' it. Tak' yer time and walk, an' no break it afore ye get it hame.' So I'd walk very slowly, holding the box fearfully, and controlling my normal bouncing step in case I'd jiggle my frail cargo to destruction.

There was quite a ceremony as Grannie and I carefully raised the lid and gazed inside to confirm that all was well. And there, suspended by its four wee lugs, which hung from neat, cut-out projections of thin cardboard, was our 'inverted gas mantle'.

It looked incredibly fragile and white, with a frosted lacy texture which trembled at a breath, and the smooth chalky neck seemed too brittle for mortal hands.

A chair was brought forward for the hanging. I envied Grannie this part intensely, and it was many years before she listened to my plea of 'Och let me put the new mantle on, Grannie.'

'You!' she would snort. 'Dae ye want it broken to smithereens afore it's in the hoose a meenute?'

It was a delicate job and called for deft fingers to hang the wee lugs safely from the matching supports of the gas bracket, and we held our breaths as Grannie moved her fingers away, for the slightest misjudgement could send the mantle shattering to the floor.

Great care was taken when the match was applied to a new mantle. Some people, in fact, burnt the whole thing with a flaming match before letting the gas in, but we never did this. The gas tap was turned on just a little, so that only a small quantity of gas whispered into the tiny globe. The match was held at just the right distance to ignite the gas, but not so close as to endanger the new surface. There was a 'Plop' as the gas caught the flame, and the lowest tip of the globe sprang to brilliant life.

Cautiously the tap was turned up and up, until the whole mantle was pulsing with light. We let our held breaths go in a sigh of satisfaction. The new mantle had been successfully broken in.

But it took a long time for me to stop feeling guilty for having caused this needless expense. Poverty is a very exacting teacher, and I had been taught well. We learned never to waste a single thing during our childhood. We were generous with what we had – no beggar was ever turned away from our door, and we could always manage a welcome cup of tea for a visitor – but we wasted nothing. When I was old enough to be trusted to empty the sugar bags into the big glass jar, Grannie showed me how to fold back the corners, first at the top, and finally at the bottom, so that it was smooth and unwrinkled and not a grain of sugar lost in any tiny crevice. The same treatment was given to the tea packets, while the butter papers were carefully scraped with a knife before being folded and put away, and Grannie used them later to cover the rice pudding or grease the baking tins.

When my mother, visiting a neighbour, would see her transferring butter from paper to dish by tapping it out, before screwing up the paper and tossing it into the fire, she would shake her head, aghast at such waste. 'All that good butter into the fire,' she would say to us later; 'nae wonder they havenae a ha'penny to their name.'

It was years before I knew anybody actually *bought* string. When a rare parcel would arrive at our house Grannie and I would sit down at the table to open it. 'We'll just tak' time tae lowse the string,' she would say. 'Never waste a good bit o' string wi' shears, for you never ken when it'll come in useful.' With unhurried fingers she would undo every knot, until she had a smooth length of string, and then she would show me how to wind it into a neat figure eight, and securely fasten it before popping it into the string bag which hung inside the cupboard door. The brown paper round the parcel was also smoothed and folded, and put away for later use, and, of course, every paper poke was smoothed and kept in a drawer for my mother's pieces for her work, or chittering bites and pieces for us.

We children of the tenements were aware of the economy of daily living. We knew food wasn't always there for the asking and we learned to know the price and value of everything. With a sixpence clutched in my hand, I would race down to the greengrocer's before breakfast. 'Sixpence-worth of vegetables for soup,' I would say, and I'd watch with eagle eye to make sure I got a wee bit of everything. Carrot, turnip, leek and some parsley. It was no use the greengrocer trying to tell me parsley was too dear today to be included in the sixpence-worth. 'You need parsley for broth,' I would say stubbornly. 'And Grannie said I was to get it with my sixpence-worth.' I usually did.

An 'outside' loaf was a farthing cheaper than one baked in the middle of the row, for it had a hard shiny outside slice which was tough and indigestible. 'Will I get an outside one?' I'd ask Grannie eagerly when coppers were scarce and pay-day a long way off. 'They're a whole farthing cheaper.' 'Nae, naw lassie,' she would say, 'it's nae savin' at a', for naebody could eat it wi' pleasure, and that slice would be wasted,' and so I learned that a bargain wasn't always a bargain, even if the price-tag was lower.

I used to trot into the town with the daughter of a neighbour, even poorer than we were, for there was a special shop which sold ham-bones for tuppence-ha'penny for two pairs, and that gave them two good pots of lentil soup, and a good picking at the bones with their boiled potatoes. It was a mile and a half each way, but we thought nothing of it, especially if it was the gird season, and we were there and back before we knew it.

I discovered gradually that a highly priced roast wasn't necessarily better than the delicious potted meats Grannie could make with the cheaper shin of beef. And I found too that boiling beef on the bone had a flavour all its own, and it didn't matter that it was a wee bit on the fat side, for that gave it added sweetness. 'Aye,' Grannie would nod approvingly, as she saw me waiting till there was just an inch of meat clinging all round before I'd hold out my plate, 'oor Molly kens what's guid for her. The sweeter the meat the nearer the bone.' And she showed me how to blow out the marrow to mix with my plain boiled potatoes, and we both remembered the words of the hymn, 'Even as with marrow and with fat my soul shall filled be'. I thoroughly agreed with hymns as practical as this.

By the time I was ten years old, Grannie could trust me to choose a piece of beef, knowing I'd bring back the very best value in the shop for the money I had to spend. I could shoulder this responsibility quite confidently when only one or two shillings were involved, but I remember one Christmas I was sent to get a piece of roast beef for our Christmas dinner, and when the butcher said 'Seven-and-six' I nearly choked in panic. I didn't know so much about roasts. What if I chose wrongly and wasted my mother's precious money? So, oblivious of the other customers, and shaking with the weight of decision, I asked the butcher to keep it aside while I ran home and described it to my grannie. 'It's like a great big chop, Grannie,' I told her breathlessly, 'with a wee bit of different colour in the middle, and a wee division of fat right here,' and I pointed to the place on the table where I was drawing it with my finger. 'And it's seven-and-six. Will I get it?'

She sat still, considering what I had said. 'Aye,' she said at last, 'get it. If it's like that, then it's sirloin, and it's a grand bit o' meat.' I flew back to the shop. 'I'll take it,' I said importantly, laying down my three half-crowns with a lordly air. It *was* sirloin. It was delicious, and Grannie gave me a special slice of the wee bit in the middle which was a different colour, and told me it was the fillet. That was a new word for me – I'd only heard of fillet fish – but I remembered it, and agreed with Grannie that it was the finest delicacy of all.

All the jam in our house was home-made. My mother's comment, 'She's the kind that aye has bought jam on the table', was enough to let us know the shiftlessness of the person she was describing. We'd watch the shop windows until the jam fruit was at its lowest price, then rush home with the news, 'Grannie, the man says the black currants'll no' get ony cheaper', or 'The strawberries are goin' up again next week.' Out would come the big purse, and off we'd scamper to get the fruit and the preserving sugar, 'And mind ye get nice dry fruit noo,' Grannie would exhort, 'Nane o' his wet sleeshy stuff or the jam'll no' set.'

When a loved mother died in our tenements the tragedy was felt by us all. But the family was never broken up and scattered to different Council homes. The father went to his work as usual, but the children, skilled shoppers and well aware of the work every penny had to do, ran the house and bought the food, and would have been astounded if anybody had suggested it was too much for them. There was no mystery in housekeeping to them. They had done the shopping since they could toddle, and could count up their change like adding machines. In our tenements it was never too early to learn to face up to life.

Five

In winter-time the Angier's emulsion didn't always work its magic, and sometimes I'd have to be kept off school because of a bronchial cold or flu. We didn't bother to call the doctor, for we were used to this sort of illness. And I loved being lifted from the hurley bed into the cool vastness of the big recess bed where my mother usually slept, but she was now off to work. It was almost worth while being ill to lie there, snug and warm, with the stir and activity of the house around me.

What a lot of things Grannie had to do when we were out at school. There were all the vegetables to be washed and scraped or peeled, and cut into tiny squares for the soup. And I never knew she fried the onion and the floured meat when she was making stew. Mmm, what a good smell the frying onion had. And how pleasant it was to watch her get out the flour and the milk, and know that in a wee while I was going to be given a lovely pancake straight off the girdle, dripping with margarine. The wifie across the landing had smelt the pancakes too, it seemed, for she came in to ask the time, as her clock had stopped, and was just able to wait to have a cup of tea with us. And then the potatoes had to be peeled and put on to boil, to be ready in time for my mother coming in from work and the boys from school, for they all got home at dinner-time. I was only hungry for a wee bowl of soup, and a beggar who came to the door also got a bowlful, for Grannie said he looked more in need of a guid bowl of soup than a penny, which she couldn't spare anyway.

But when Grannie herself was ill, things were very different. She suffered from severe bronchitis, and every winter the doctor had to come to see her. I was usually kept off school to let him in, and the fuss that went on before his visit astonished me. The night before, my mother flew about laying out clean sheets and pillow-cases, and a clean nightie for Grannie. A fresh cloth was placed in readiness for the table. The range was polished, the floor swept, and the brass covers burnished till they hung in a gleaming row above the dresser, the coal fire reflected in every one of them.

The morning of the visit, my mother rose an hour earlier than she usually did. The bed was stripped, Grannie was put into the fresh nightie and laid gently against the splendid snowy pillow, hardly daring to breathe in case she'd crumple it before the doctor arrived. I sponged her face and hands while my mother put finishing touches to the bed-cover, and smoothed the gathers of the bed-pawn, and then, when she had made sure everything was really in mint condition, off went Mother to work. She was well satisfied the doctor wouldn't find a flaw anywhere, as far as material things went.

I busied myself getting the dinner ready under Grannie's sharp directions. She had small patience with slackness, sickbed or no, and woe betide me if I used the wrong-sized spoon for anything, or stopped stirring till she told me the exact moment.

At last came the knock at the door. My heart in my mouth, I would gaze at Grannie.

'Will I open it?' I would whisper.

'Of course. Do you think you're going to keep him on the landing? Ask him to come in, and then don't open your mouth to say a word till he goes away.'

My cheeks flushed with nervousness, my mouth dry with fright, I'd turn the handle, and there on the landing was the doctor. A huge man carrying a wee black bag. 'Come in,' I would whisper, 'Grannie's in her bed in the kitchen.'

A pair of blue eyes would take in the neat, tidy, immaculate kitchen, and with a twinkling smile he would advance towards the bed and, to my horror, actually *sit* on my mother's good bed-cover. *Nobody* was allowed to sit on this! Grannie would flash me a warning glance when she heard my gasp of dismay. The doctor would speak. 'Now, now, Grannie, what have you been up to, eh?' I was sure Grannie would give him the rough edge of her tongue for daring to suggest she had been up to anything, but she was smiling and preening herself and, surprisingly, not the least bit angry.

Her chest was impressively sounded, and the wee black things he had worn in his ears were put away in the bag. A prescription was written out and left on the table and then, before I realized it, he had patted me on the head and was out of the door. The visit was over.

'Now,' Grannie would say, all satisfaction that everything had gone off so well, and I hadn't done anything to disgrace her, 'we'll hae a wee cup o' tea. A nice chiel yon, and real clever. I've never kent a doctor who gave a better bottle.'

'A chiel,' I'd repeat to myself, puzzled at such a description. He seemed like a very old man to me. He was strange and fierce, with his queer prescriptions written in an unknown hand, bold and free with his careless crumpling of my mother's best bed-cover, and greatly to be feared with his wee black bag. But Grannie was certainly right about the good bottles he prescribed, for it only needed one visit and one bottle to have Grannie on her feet again, and when Grannie was well we could all dare to be cheeky again, and I could get back to my rightful place in the hurley bed again, and coorie into her back.

But och I was glad that our grannie only had bronchitis when she had to have the doctor, for there was another old lady in the tenements who was 'dotted' as we called the mentally ill, and the doctor had to prescribe a different sort of bottle to keep her safe and quiet.

She was very old – about eighty, Grannie said – with snow-white hair, a pink wrinkled skin, light blue eyes with an expression of bewildered innocence which made her look like an elderly baby, and a high sing-song voice. She was the mother of neighbours who used to live downstairs in our tenement, and Grannie had known her in her saner days. So when the family moved away, and nobody in the new tenement could be bothered with her, it was to our house she found her way almost daily.

I was about eleven years old at the time, and the number of times I had to take Grannie Mackay all the way back to her house were beyond counting. No question of riding on a tramcar or a bus either, for there was no money for such extras. Walk we must and walk we did.

How she found her way to our house without coming to grief in the heavy traffic was a mystery. When I would come home from school I would whisper to my grannie, 'Is she here?', and my heart would sink into a gloom of fear at the reply, 'Don't stand there on the mat – of course she's here, and she's lookin' furrit to seeing you.'

One of Grannie Mackay's more frightening habits was her inconsistency in the matter of sex. 'Here's Molly to see you,' my grannie would call out cheerfully. Old Mrs Mackay would fix me with a surprised blue eye, as though I didn't live in our house. 'Oh she's a fine boy, a fine boy,' she'd chant. 'I'm *not* a boy,' I'd mutter furiously, but this tactlessness was silenced by a quenching look from my grannie. 'Aye,' the chant would continue, 'a fine boy she is, a lovely boy she is, growing every day.'

My back would be pressed against the dresser to get as far away from the old lady as possible – her witlessness frightened me, but my grannie would have none of this timidity. 'Mrs Mackay wants you to comb her hair,' she'd say briskly. This was the thing I feared most. 'Oh, Grannie,' I'd whisper tearfully, 'I don't like combing her hair. It's cold, and it feels wet and her head's all pink.'

Grannie dismissed my distaste with 'What does it matter about *your* comfort? Doesn't Mrs Mackay need her hair combed? It's little enough she has to please her. She likes you to comb her hair, and at her age her feelings are far more important than yours.' So I would climb on to the back of the big chair and with trembling fingers undo the pins and quietly brush and comb the lank white hair. Old Mrs Mackay kept up a dreamy chant as I brushed, 'Och there is lovely, it is. Och she's a fine boy at the hairdressing. A fine boy.' This would irritate me so much I'd want to give the old head a smart tap with the brush, fear or no fear, but my grannie's watchfulness prevented any such tantrums. 'What does it matter whether she thinks you're a boy or not,' Grannie would say afterwards, 'you *ken* you're a lassie, and calling you a boy isn't going to turn you into one!'

At last the moment would arrive when Grannie would say 'Now, Mrs Mackay, your daughter will be wondering where you are, and your tea will be ready. Molly will take you home.'

With great ceremony she would don her grey shawl, place her black 'mutch' over her carefully combed hair, and rise panting and grunting to her feet. Obeying a nod from Grannie, I'd draw old Mrs Mackay's arm

88

through mine, and lead her slowly – oh, how slowly – out of the house, down the stairs, into the street and along the road through the traffic to her daughter's house. As often as not, I'd hardly be home again when she was back almost at my heels, having completely forgotten she'd just left us. Back we'd go again, and I'd whisper to her relatives that they must try to keep her in, because I'd homework to do and I couldn't be running back and forward all night. My grannie would have been furious had she heard me, but I felt I *had* to make a stand somewhere.

But if the clouded mind of the 'dotted' frightened me, the mere whisper of 'fever', that infant scourge, sent our mothers sick with dread. With twelve families to a close, infection could spread like wildfire, and the sight of the fever van struck a chill into our hearts. But curiosity among us children was always stronger than fear and we would gather on the pavement to catch a glimpse of a swathed figure on its way through the close to the ambulance, and shudder with relief that it wasn't us on the stretcher. Awed as we children were by the sight of our playmate magically transformed to a terrifying bundle, borne by two solemn ambulancemen, we realized that while we were lively and healthy we might as well enjoy ourselves, and give a bit of help at the same time. So we organized back-court concerts to raise money to buy presents for the hospital cases.

As soon as the ambulance had disappeared we'd race through the close to the back court and decide on our entertainment. We'd maybe arrange to do an imitation of the pantomime we'd seen from the gallery during the winter, or a cowboys and Indians episode from the latest film, and we had to decide whether our costumes would be made from crinkled paper or cast-offs begged from our mothers. We'd divide out the roles to be played, and we sewed and pinned and rehearsed for days, practically in a fever ourselves as we got everything ready for the performance. We never repeated a show. It had to be a full-scale new production for each victim, and we lived every minute of it.

We charged a ha'penny for children and a penny for adults, and the adults sat on the stone edging which ran round the back-court railings. The children sat on the ground or stood, just as they pleased. We generally gave two performances, and our audience usually stayed for both, and were highly critical if they didn't get an exact repeat performance at the second house, word for word, gesture for gesture. As nothing was written down and everything had been rehearsed on the principle of 'You say this' and 'I'll say that', this wasn't easy, but we pacified them by singing an extra verse of a favourite song if the mood turned too critical.

Although I was always very nervous, I was quite drunk with power when I discovered how easy it was to change the mood of an audience from one of enthusiastic noisy delight at my swash-buckling impersonation of a Principal Boy, to silent pathos at my rendering of 'Won't you buy my pretty flowers'. Heady stuff, and I quite forgot the victim in my enthusiastic production of my all-talking, all-singing, all-dancing extravaganzas.

We usually collected enough in pennies and ha'pennies to be able to offer the fever victim a huge box of chocolates and a bag of fruit, and the shopping expeditions were themselves a source of intense pleasure. We felt like millionaires as we crowded into the sweet-shop and selected, with great care, a box with a sympathetic dog on the lid, and then moved to the fruit-shop next door, where we spent the rest of the money on as many apples and oranges as the kitty would cover. No fanciful things like grapes or melons for us – oranges and apples were our limit and we knew they would be appreciated to the last bite.

Somehow one always assumed it would be somebody else who would be chosen for the victim, and the part of the entertainer would be filled by oneself.

And then, one year when we simply couldn't afford it to happen, the fever germ struck our house, and it struck me. My aunt was home on a visit from Australia on a specially reduced ticket which involved her travelling back by a certain date. If she went beyond this date an extra twenty pounds had to be paid, an enormous sum in our world, in fact an impossible sum for us to find. She had come home to have her last baby born in Scotland, and was within three weeks of her sailing date when I came in complaining of a sore throat and a throbbing head. I didn't know what those symptoms meant, but my mother and my grannie did. I caught the look of horror which passed between them and I was puzzled. They didn't speak, beyond handing me a glass, pouring in some stuff and telling me to gargle. As I was tucked into bed, I heard Auntie whisper, 'We ought to send for the doctor.' My mother shushed her fiercely. 'We can't. You'd never be allowed to leave, and you must get that boat. Where could we get twenty pounds.' 'But, Jeanie,' my auntie urged, 'she should be in hospital.' Hospital! Ambulances! I was to be the next bundle carried through the awe-struck spectators! I felt tears sting my eyelids at the thought of it, but my mother would have none of it. 'I can do what's necessary,' she said.

Now at that time in our small room-and-kitchen tenement dwelling there were three adults, three children and an infant; an outside toilet had to be shared with two other families, so the risk of spreading infection was terrifying. But my mother faced it all, and took it in her stride. She was used to hardship, and to battling with difficulties, with poverty a powerful spur, and in this crisis she was magnificent.

She had her job in the big engineering works to attend to, but she saw that everything I touched or used was sterilized. She was so dramatic when she explained to my brothers about the dangers of using anything I had eaten from that for months afterwards they refused to drink from a cup if they'd seen it anywhere near my bed during my illness. Towels and face-flannel were kept scrupulously apart from the others, gargling routines punctiliously observed, light diet adhered to, and as I slept with Grannie we felt it wasn't very likely she would be infected at her age.

The worst part was trying to keep my school chums from visiting me. We couldn't and daren't tell them the real cause of my illness, but we couldn't risk suspicion and the dreaded 'sanitary' inspector descending upon us by refusing everyone admittance. So the one or two special chums who couldn't be kept out were made to sit at the other end of the kitchen, by the window, and yell their sympathy from there, on the excuse that I was very easily made sneeze, and the cold air they brought in with them sent me off on an attack if they sat too close to me. Strange to say, everybody believed this. We were a trusting community. Even I wasn't sure that it was fever I had, for the word was never mentioned, until the skin began to peel in strips from my hands. Then I wore little white silk gloves and pretended this was to keep my hands warm when I kept them outside the clothes, which I liked, for if they got cold it made me sneeze again. Once more, because I'd always been full of mad capers and loved dressing up, everybody believed us.

The new baby was kept in the other room, and I never saw her again, except held at a distance at the other end of the kitchen just before she left with Auntie for the boat. Auntie gazed at me compassionately and lovingly, but didn't dare come closer to say goodbye.

It was a miracle, of course, but nobody on the stair developed even the mildest symptom. I gradually found my strength, and at last was ready for school again. My absence had been explained as prolonged bronchitis, and as I was always top of the class and an enthusiastic pupil, nobody doubted us. But there was a terrible moment when I went back to school and the teacher looked up from the register as I answered 'Present, miss'. 'Oh, hullo. Are you better? Was it fever?'

I stared at her dumbly, the blood rushing to my pale cheeks. 'How had she guessed? What would I say?' It was one thing acting a lie, especially when I hadn't really known it was a lie for a long time. It was quite another thing putting it into words. Then she consulted the register again, with its marginal notes. 'Oh no, bronchitis, I see. Are you sure you're better? You look very congested to me.' Congested! I was on the point of fainting with fear, followed by relief.

So even into the school register our deception had succeeded. Succeeded so well, in fact, that I didn't have a single 'benefit' concert. No chocolates or fruit for bronchitis. Only for scarlet fever, and I hadn't had that. Or had I?

But if I hadn't had the chocolates, I hadn't had the ride in the dreaded 'fever van' either. Nor had anybody else in our house, or in our tenement during that epidemic anyway.

But that was a terrible risk my mother took.

Although we only had a room and a kitchen for the five of us, we never felt overcrowded, for our accommodation was palatial compared with many of the tenement families. There were several large families living in a single room in our neighbourhood, or at best a single room with a tiny apartment opening out of it, not much bigger than a pantry. This small box-like room was considered a luxury to be envied by those who had to crowd into a single room, and they dreamed of what good use they could put the extra space.

One family in our tenement had fourteen children and they all lived in one room with just this small box-like compartment leading out of it, and once they actually held a wedding reception there when the eldest daughter was married. As the younger children came in from play, they quietly crawled under the festive table and vanished into the smaller room, where bags of chips were handed through to them, and they boasted of this treat for weeks afterwards. Long experience of living in such cramped conditions had trained them to play noiselessly and happily, and they might have been a family of mice for all the noise they made. Indeed some of the wedding guests never even knew they were there.

In all the years of my childhood, I never knew that family's mother's voice raised in anger. And the wedding feast was the only occasion I ever saw her without her working apron. On this one glorious night her eyes could be lifted above the level of the kitchen sink, and the bridal pair were waved off in a shower of confetti to their own little single end, which they had miraculously found ten minutes away, so visiting mother and the thirteen brothers and sisters would be no problem.

Farther along the street, another family of fourteen had a room and kitchen like ours, separated by a lobby, and both rooms of equal size. They felt they were so rich in space that they added to their meagre income by taking in a lodger. This was a great source of interest and mystery to me. I'd never heard of a lodger before, and viewed this man as somebody very special. He was on constant night-shift, which meant he slept during the day. None of us saw anything unusual in the fact that he surely slept in a bed which was used at night by several of the fourteen other occupants who, of course, slept at the normal time during the night. I thought this a most resourceful arrangement, making a bed earn its keep in this convenient way.

As I was friendly with one of the daughters in this exciting household, I used to pay occasional visits there, and I must have embarrassed the lodger terribly, sitting staring at him with unwinking eye, noting every detail of his appearance, from his thick thatch of red hair to his heavy-soled tackety boots, careful to overlook nothing in the personality of this strange being, the first lodger I had ever seen.

The common factor to such large households was their quietness. This amazed me. I was too young to realize that where three children could be naturally exuberant, twelve or fourteen just had to be quiet and restrained or anarchy would have prevailed. And it was easy to see how fond they all were of each other. In the house where there were fourteen, the girl I was friendly with told me in all seriousness that when the oldest son was married they felt the house was empty. They missed him so much, they could hardly bear it. I'd have thought they would have been grateful for a little extra breathing space, but their minds didn't run that way.

With these examples of ingenuity all round us we didn't even stop to think twice where the wedding celebrations would be held when my mother's youngest sister got married. We'd have them in our house, of course, in the evening, after a five o'clock wedding so that all the men could be present. There was no question of anybody asking time off work for anything so frivolous as a wedding, so the festive board would have to wait till they'd finished their day's work and changed out of their dungarees into their Sunday dark suits. My mother and her sister shared the costs, and of course it could all be supplied on credit on our Cooperative book, and the dividend on such a huge expense would be as good as winning a sweepstake. We knew about such things for my mother shared a sixpenny ticket with a workmate on Derby Day, and she had once won twenty-five shillings – a fortune.

Although my mother had thrown up her hands in amazement at the wedding which had been held in the close, with its slit of a boxroom for the children, she wasn't in the least daunted by the thought of having to arrange for all the eating, drinking and entertaining to take place in our one good room. Or of only having one wee kitchen for the coats, and the washing up and where

Grannie and I would be sleeping. Or that the toilet arrangements were one flight of stairs down, and we were adding at least two dozen to the two families already sharing this amenity. She took such difficulties in her stride, and we all plunged into our various tasks with a will.

Everything that could be stowed out of sight was pushed under beds, or crammed into wardrobes and chests of drawers, and I may say that we had a fine time afterwards trying to find clothes for bed that night and for school next morning.

About four o'clock in the afternoon, long trestle tables arrived and were set up, one along each side wall and one across the oriel window, and long benches were ranged behind each table to give seating accommodation to the greatest number that could be squeezed into the room. We had burst the bank and were having outside caterers, and we children rushed in and out among the workmen's feet, delirious with joy at the transformation scene which turned our one and only parlour into a little hall before our very eyes.

Long boards filled with crockery and glasses were brought in, and the places set on snowy white table-cloths, also supplied by the caterer. We'd never seen such vast pieces of linen, and shuddered with horror at the thought of tea being spilled on such dazzling cloths, for we couldn't imagine how long it must take to wash and dry cloths of that size, or how they could ever be ironed to such a state of smooth perfection. As we stared, fervently praying we wouldn't be the ones to disgrace ourselves with such a mishap, the next contingent were bustling in, carrying boards filled with plates of sliced bread, cakes and biscuits. These were ranged along the tables, and bottles of sauce and pickles placed at strategic intervals and, after a long critical survey to make sure nothing had been overlooked, vases of flowers were moved from the sideboard and laid exactly in the centre of each table.

Next came the drinks, which were left in a corner of the kitchen, ready to be opened at the appropriate moment.

As we lived two flights of stairs from the street, you can imagine the amount of tramping up and down that took place during this non-stop performance, but everybody loved a wedding and there wasn't a word of complaint from neighbours or workmen.

By five o'clock it was pandemonium, with my mother trying to get the three of us children dressed, not forgetting helping Grannie into her black silk blouse with the cameo brooch at the collar, and endeavouring to shake the creases out of her own lilac crêpe, which had been knocked off the hook at the back of the door three times by the men as they pushed past delivering another load of food.

We didn't go to the ceremony, as my mother was terrified to leave the house in case something calamitous would happen, so we had a little extra time for dressing. But the last button was barely done up when bride and groom were with us, and guests pouring in behind them, shrugging out of coats and hats, and making their way to the room where the laden tables glittered and gleamed under the gas chandelier which was my mother's pride and joy.

There was much praise for the beauty of the arrangements, and a good deal of jostling and squeezing as people wriggled into their places. Then, with perfect timing, the waitresses arrived to serve the meal. Ahead of them four men strode in, bearing boards of steak pies and vegetables. We children yelled with delight. Never had we seen so many pies all at once, never such gigantic mounds of snowy mashed potatoes, never such tureens of peas, never such vast bowls of mashed swedes.

There was some slight embarrassment in having strange waitresses standing over us as we ate, but it was a bitterly cold night and we quickly forgot them as we tucked into our delicious meal, and soon toasts were being drunk to great bursts of laughter, much of which was beyond the children, and then the tables were dismantled and the floor cleared for singing, games and dancing.

The vocalists needed a bit of coaxing before they'd agree to sing us a favourite song, and my Uncle Johnnie was furious because his wife insisted on singing soulfully 'The March of the Cameron Men'. He felt she was parading her pride in him too openly. This was because he had been a Cameron Highlander in the war!

Grannie sang, in imitation of Victorian music-hall

ballad, 'Be kind to auld Grannie, for noo she is frail, like a time-shattered tree bending low in the Gale', and I wept copiously because I thought the words were so touching and so beautiful. Somebody else sang 'O' a' the airts the wind can blaw', and my mother wept, and we all had a lovely time.

We played forfeits, and bee baw babbity and games involving wee bits of paper and pencil. And then we had an eightsome reel, and quadrilles, and there wasn't a cheep of protest from the family living underneath.

The door of our house was wide open most of the evening, and anybody who felt like it was welcome to come in and see the bride and toast her health. The fun went on till midnight, and when at last they all departed, our faces were flushed with triumph and happiness, for we had had a wonderful wedding. 'A great celebration, Jeannie,' they said to my mother as they left. 'A splendid repast and a grand wedding.'

Looking back, I realized all this must have involved an enormous amount of work for my mother, and it must have taken days to get cleared up in spite of help from caterers. But they were unsophisticated times, and a passionate belief in our ability to put on a show helped to make the work light. And for many moons afterwards, whenever anyone mentioned any grand occasion, I always countered with 'Just like my auntie's wedding, when we had real waitresses in our house and thousands of steak pies'.

Six

When I was a wee girl if you said that something looked 'hand-made' it was the greatest insult you could hurl at the disparaged article. To be exactly the same as everyone else was the look that was coveted, and great was the anguish suffered by children whose mothers had to make do and mend from anything which came to hand.

Luckily I didn't mind a bit, which was just as well, for I don't think my mother was ever able to afford a single garment which the school required. Apart from my boots, which, of course, had to be bought because none of us had figured out how to make them from anything lying around the house, practically everything was hand-made, and mostly out of things first worn by my mother or somebody else. The endless hours and patience which must have gone into fashioning my garments weren't met with a scowl by me, for I was well aware of the tightness of the family budget.

Grannie knitted my long black stockings, and I took as much pride as she did in the 'intakes' at the back, which made the shape and could truly be described as 'fully-fashioned'. How well they clung to my ankles, and rose long and snug right to the tops of my legs, where they met the buttons on my Liberty bodice.

When her tweed skirt was beyond hope for her own use, it was cunningly fashioned into a little pleated skirt for me, and we both thought I was elegance itself when this was topped with an exactly matching woollen jumper Grannie knitted. This wool we got from somebody who worked in a wool warehouse, and it was going practically free because it had become entangled, and the firm couldn't waste time rewinding it. A great bargain this. In fact I wore this particular jumper for years, with Grannie cleverly changing the collar each winter. One year it sported a grey angora collar, the next a red and white striped one, and latterly a white rabbit's wool one. I was elated when my schoolteacher said in its final winter, 'Another new jumper from your grannie's clever needles?', and I was able to say demurely, but proudly, 'No, miss, just a new collar.' And I never forgot that lesson, that it is amazingly easy to ring the changes on an old garment by a new eye-catching accessory.

We saw nothing frumpty in wearing 'winter combs'. They were cosy and comforting in wintry weather, both indoors and out, for in spite of the coal fire in the range, it could be cold in the tenements. Grannie was able to knit us lovely cosy combs in pale grey or pale pink, buying the wool in bulk through that same good fairy in the wool warehouse. I don't think I ever saw Grannie without her steel needles flashing in her lap, summer or winter, for it was a constant task keeping us all clothed all the year round.

She was an expert knitter, and I remember my mother being fascinated by a little waistcoat she saw in a pattern book, and beginning to knit this in brown and mustard shades. Grannie took one look at the size and said, 'That will fit oor Molly when it's feenished, but never you, it's far ower wee.' My mother was indignant for she had implicit faith that a book must be far more accurate than Grannie's invented patterns. Doggedly she followed the instructions, pressed out the finished garment and sewed it together. We all looked at each other, and my mother walked out of the kitchen without a word. I felt so sorry that it had turned out this way after all her hard work, for she wasn't a natural knitter like Grannie, but I must say that sporty little waistcoat kept my back snug and warm for a good few winters, and in the end my mother rejoiced that at least she had made a first-class job of this tiny garment. 'You'd think it had been bought in a shop,' she said proudly. 'You'd never think it had been hand-made.'

My summer ginghams were devised from about a yard of material at elevenpence ha'penny or one shilling and sixpence, and, of course, not a penny was spent on a pattern. My mother just copied whatever style took her fancy. Boys' clothes had to be bought, you see, for the first attempt to make a pair of trousers was so disastrous that a second was never even contemplated. The boys were far more conventional than I was, and utterly refused to be dressed differently from their fellows. But with a girl it was different – for I didn't mind my slightly unusual clothes. Mind you, dresses were easy, and with this girl it was certainly different, I'd been reading quite a lot about a little French girl who came to stay in Scotland, and who looked completely different from everyone else and went sobbing to bed each night because of this; but in the end she triumphed, because a rich lady came and instantly picked out this little oddity because she was elegant and *chic*, and not ordinary like the others, and she took her on a splendid holiday to the seaside. This story reinforced Grannie's teaching that it didn't matter if one looked different from other people, and in fact at times could be a positive advantage. Alas, no rich lady picked me out from the crowd, but the upstairs neighbours did take me with them when they went to the sea in the summer, after I'd had flu, and that was almost as good.

When the time came for me to move to the higher school we were at our wits' end, for now it was demanded that I wear a gym tunic with a blouse underneath. Where on earth could we find the money for a gym tunic? Even the coarsest serge was beyond my mother's pocket. She looked over her meagre wardrobe. She had a fine navy gaberdine jacket and skirt, and decided she'd sacrifice the skirt for me. This time I was in a panic, for I'd been told it *had* to be serge. How could gaberdine look like serge? It was much finer, and it was a slightly lighter shade of navy, and this time I just had to be the same as the rest of the class. It was a uniform. I was certain I wouldn't be allowed to study with the rest of the class, and would be condemned to the junior school for ever.

My mother ignored my anguished cries and sewed on. When I saw the finished result I sat down and wept. Not only was it a light navy, not only gaberdine, but with the curve of the skirt she hadn't been able to make a square yoke; and the pleats were hung on to a curved yoke, the square corners rounded instead of sharp. Added to this, my mother had decided the best value in blouses was Tussore silk, not white cotton. Not only was it cheap, but it wouldn't show the dirt, an important consideration. I crept to school that first day, hardly daring to take off my coat. To my amazement, half the girls in the new class had no gym tunics at all. The teacher cast an inquiring eye over us, and then asked me to come out to the front. My moment of shame was upon me. I could hardly see for threatening tears, and my face was red as a beetroot. My very ears were tingling. And through my confusion I heard her say, 'Now that's the sort of neat appearance I would like all of you to achieve. You can have a choice of blouse, so long as the colours are pale, but you can see what a neat uniform appearance you will present when you're all dressed like this.' I went back to my seat in a dream. She hadn't minded at all about the gaberdine – or the curved yoke – or the Tussore silk blouse. My mother was delighted when I told her that I'd been brought out in front of the whole class to let everybody see the homemade gym tunic, which was an example of what the others should attempt. 'Aye,' she said happily, 'I'll bet she never realized it was home-made.'

Everyone else had satchels or leather cases, but not me. When the old satchel I'd inherited from somebody else at last fell to bits, just as I was transferring to the higher school, a man in my mother's workshop in the Railways made me a perfect little case of wood, and even added a little plate to it with my name. It was stained dark brown, and it seemed to me *far* better than leather, because I could stand on it in emergency without harming it a bit, and it could be buffed up with boot polish to a gleaming mahogany shade. I liked its originality and I liked its stout strength, and I loved its little name-plate.

For the final school party, when I was about to leave that school, Mother and I racked our brains to concoct something which would be worthy of the dux of the school. We were as hard up as ever, of course, so it would have to be something we could make from the simplest of materials. A stroll past Margaret Hunter's, then the best children's shop in Glasgow, revealed a dream of a dress in the window, composed of yards and yards of narrow frilling and looking like the fairy on top of the Xmas tree. My mother stared at it intently, counting the rows, observing how the neckline was cut, how the sleeves fitted, where the waist was darted.

She counted the money in her purse, went next door to a big emporium stocking all sorts of materials, and came out with a huge parcel, bulky but very light to carry. 'Aye this will take me a' ma time,' she observed, 'for it will all have to be sewn in separate rows, but I think I can manage it for the party.' Every night when she came in from work she'd stitch those frills with tiny perfect strokes, and I'd hang over her, counting how many we still had to go before we could start shaping it into a dress. At last she had enough and we could pin it to its muslin base.

The night before the party I tried it on. It was perfect. My cheeks were flushed with pleasure, especially as my mother had somehow managed to add the last touch of elegance – a silver bow with narrow streamers fastening off the neckline. The party of course was a joy. Lots to eat, splendid games, prizes to be collected, and school holidays to follow. When I came home my mother was waiting. 'Well?' she asked. 'Mother,' I burst out, 'my teacher asked me if you'd bought my dress from Margaret Hunter's.' We stared at each other. A great smile spread over my mother's tired face. 'Margaret Hunter's,' she said dreamily. 'Aye, I never thought in my wildest dreams my home-made dress would be mistaken for a shop one. It was well worth the effort, well worth it.'

All of us in the tenements took great care of our clothes. We knew how hard they were to come by, and we changed out of our school clothes the minute we reached home, without having to be told. We all had tough hand-knitted jerseys which the girls wore over tweed skirts, and the boys over old trousers for back-court games, while for Sundays and special visiting to relatives and friends we had a 'best' outfit, which we guarded and cared for like mink. How splendid those Sunday clothes seemed as we laid them out on the bed, before getting ready for church or Sunday School. The boys, in their dashing sailor suits, seemed like entirely different creatures from their wild weekday selves, as they walked sedately on either side of me.

In summer I felt elegant beyond belief in a neat navy suit, Tussore silk blouse, little white socks and flat lacing shoes. Sometimes the shoes varied a little, and might have a strap across the instep, but whether strap or laces, they magically seemed to lend grace to my legs which, during the week, knew only the stout support of long lacing boots. Our mothers were firmly convinced that boots kept young ankles well shaped and supported, and who knows they may have been right, for certainly all of us seemed to have limbs like race-horses with trim, strong ankles.

In winter the suits were carefully brushed and put to the back of the wardrobe, and out came the heavy coats for the boys and myself. From the box on top of the wardrobe my black velour hat was brought out, and its elastic checked for strength and stretchiness, to make sure it would stay firmly anchored at all times. In church a favourite pastime during a dull sermon was to draw the elastic in a wide Vee out from the chin, and let it fly with a satisfactory 'ping' over the lips. We had to be careful though, for a too-loud twanging noise brought a sharp rap on the head from the nearest adult.

We didn't seem to grow very fast, for I remember

wearing the same clothes year in, year out. Mind you, they had been prudently bought 'for growth', and were only replaced when the last inch of hem had been let down, and the last tuck removed from the sleeves.

Even in our frugal district, though, there were the feckless ones. There were also those so unskilled that they knew long stretches of unemployment. The children of such families wore their school clothes for back-court games, for they had no others to change into, and they gradually reached a state of shabbiness and tatters which were considered a disgrace by the teachers. At last a day arrived when the unkempt ones would be called out to the teacher's desk, and questions whispered about their financial position.

Poor as we all were, we were fiercely independent, and we others, sitting safely at our desks, decently clad in well-preserved school clothes, would lower our eyes in sympathy for our ragged playmates. We knew the teacher was going to offer a form of application for 'Parish clothes' and we shuddered. The Parish clothes were made from scratchy woollen material, with a built-in itchy quality which made them agony to wear, and the genius who thought up the dull grey porridgy colour should have had a medal for successful depression of the human spirit. These clothes were instantly recognizable by their ugliness and harsh durability, and anyone unfortunate enough to have to wear them avoided the rest of us in the playground, in case a tactless enemy might jeer the hated words 'Parish clothes'.

We each of us rejoiced that our own parents were thrifty and such good managers that we could wear our own clothes, washed and mended and let down though they often were, with pride and ownership. To have to be dependent on the Parish for clothes seemed to us a fate worse than death.

But if we liked to wear our own clothes and buy our own jotters we had no qualms about accepting the splendid slates which the school provided. There were slots at the back of our desks where we slid the slates when we'd finished with them, and an almighty clatter they made when we pushed them home at the end of the lesson.

An old slate pencil, broken into use, was a great joy, but a new one, light grey and chalky looking, didn't seem right at all until it had been wiped clean of its powdery bloom by our clutching fingers, and was smooth and black and shiny and entirely satisfactory as it skimmed over the slate.

Sometimes a piece of grit made the pencil squeak abominably, and my teeth would grate and my spine shudder at the piercing sound. A new one was hurriedly produced by the teacher, without even having to ask, for she was even more sensitive to this scraping than we were.

On wintry days the slate struck chill on the hand which leaned on it, and a jersey sleeve made a comforting layer between hand and slate when it was pulled down snugly over the fingers. In summer a moist palm left little shadows of steamy darkness on the slate, and made it difficult for us to write.

Unlike the teacher with her blackboard, we didn't have velvet pads for wiping the slate clean. Hideously smelling damp sponges or damp flannels were kept by each of us in little tin boxes, usually discarded tobacco or sweetie tins, depending on whether they'd been begged from dads or grannies. These cloths were supposed to be damped with water before we left home, but as often as not we forgot. Then there was many a surreptitious spit to get them wet enough to wipe our slates, and they must have harboured germs by the million. In the course of time the damp contents rusted the inside of the boxes, and the smell was awful. Somehow one grew used to the peculiar odour of one's own sponge when the lid was opened, and it was only when the nose twitched at the whiff of a neighbour's box that the pungent aroma seemed revolting. I remember my favourite tin box was a beautiful pale blue which had once held Grannie's Christmas butterscotch, and Grannie allowed me, as a special favour, to cut off a piece of our soft new sponge to match this splendid container, instead of the wee bit of flannel clout I usually carried. With what pride I flourished my box as I drew it from my desk each morning, and I was convinced it was the envy of the class.

I loved my slate. Compared with Vere Foster, with its ink and its ruled lines which allowed no mistake to go unnoticed, there was something almost light-hearted in working with materials which could so easily be corrected, with no trace left to tell the tale. Vere Foster had a perfection and a discipline which reduced the whole room to utter silence while we laboured to achieve the copper-plate writing it demanded. The top line showed a virtuous sentiment in perfect handwriting, 'Honesty is the best policy', 'A burnt child fears the fire', 'Virtue is its own reward', or 'Practice makes perfect'. On the ruled lines immediately below, we had to copy the sentence, using fine up-strokes and heavy down-strokes, and this exercise was to instruct us in the art of beautiful handwriting. There was no rubbing out tolerated, for we used ink, and you could have danced to the rhythm of our pounding hearts as we toiled, terrified to spoil this beautiful exercise book.

Slates were a blessed relief after such a strain. A wee bit of a spit, and who could guess that you'd had second thoughts about that sum, or this spelling? It was the perfect embodiment of the second chance, and it seemed to me wonderfully generous of the schools to lend us such an enjoyable instrument of learning.

We always had Bible teaching first thing in the morning at school, and one of the phrases which greatly puzzled me was 'entertaining angels unaware'. How could anybody be unaware of entertaining an angel, I thought? Surely they would be instantly recognizable by their beautiful white wings, and the clouds of glory round their heads? It never occurred to me that angelic qualities could be found in the most unlikely guises, hiding under very ordinary voices and in bustling every-day bodies.

My angel, as it turned out, hid inside the little figure of my school-teacher, Miss McKenzie. To me she was always a little old lady, with her roly-poly plumpness, her slightly bowed legs, grey hair framing a round rosy face and caught up in an old-fashioned bun on top of her head. Steady blue-grey eyes watched us all shrewdly from behind gold-rimmed spectacles, and although her voice was soft and seldom raised, she kept us all in firm control.

She seemed so ancient that I was astounded to hear her say one morning, in quiet explanation when she was a few minutes late, that she had been delayed waiting for the doctor to call to attend to her mother. Her mother! Surely she must be about a hundred! In my surprise at discovering such an old lady as my teacher could have a mother still alive, it never crossed my mind to wonder how she managed to look after such an ancient parent, and cope with the exhausting task of teaching every day. And a marvellous teacher she was. She had the gift of exciting us to desire knowledge for its own sake, quite apart from that needed for examinations, and our reading went far beyond the humdrum authors we'd have found for ourselves, if left to our own devices.

I, a natural born swot, was a great favourite of hers. This was a mixed blessing, which rather embarrassed me, for 'teacher's pet' was an insult in the tenements.

Miss McKenzie refused to be kept at arm's length though, for she seemed to sense something in me which needed encouragement. She was greatly surprised to discover, when we acted out our little bits of Shakespeare, that I had a passionate interest in the theatre. She knew, of course, that my mother was a widow with few pennies to spare for theatres, so she it was who took me to a matinée one marvellous Saturday, to see Shakespeare performed as it ought to be, in a real theatre in the town.

It felt very strange to be meeting Miss McKenzie at the tram-stop, dressed in my best coat, and the tammy Grannie had knitted. I was terrified any of my school friends would see us and jeer 'Teacher's pet', which might put my teacher off the whole idea of taking me to the theatre, but mercifully they were all at the penny matinée, so we were safe. Although I felt a bit ill-at-ease sitting so close to her on the tram seat, I had to say something, so I launched into an account of how my mother had read my teacup the night before and had predicted a disappointment for me, and I'd prayed that the disappointment might not be that something would prevent us from seeing Shakespeare. Miss McKenzie seemed to have trouble with a cough just then, and even had to wipe her eyes, and I wondered if she was laughing at me. When I told Grannie about this later she was scandalized that I'd told my teacher about us believing in teacup fortunes. 'She'll think we're a lot o' heathens,' declared Grannie. 'When'll ye learn to haud yer tongue.'

Although I basked in Miss McKenzie's approval, I never really felt very close to her. We all held our teachers in some awe, and it never dawned on me to ask her advice as to what I should do when I left school. Surely there was only one thing to do? Get a job and earn money to add to the household purse as quickly as possible. What sort of job? Oh, if only I were lucky enough, it could be the Cooperative offices, a highly prized post in our district. I'd start as an office girl, and go to night classes to try to master the mysteries of office routine. If I couldn't get in there it would have to be a shop.

But Miss McKenzie had other ideas. We in our house knew nothing of scholarships for fatherless children. The idea of a child from a working-class household going to college was the very stuff of story-books, and had nothing to do with the business of living as we knew it.

Unknown to us, she bullied the headmaster into putting my name forward for a special scholarship open to children who showed some promise, and who would benefit from further education. As I was the school dux, he agreed, although he was a bit worried about the expense of keeping me at college for a whole year from my mother's point of view. No earnings from me, and fare and clothes to be covered, for, of course, only the fees would be paid if I won.

Miss McKenzie brushed all argument aside. She came herself with me to the interview with the scholarship board. My mother couldn't get time off work for such a wild-cat scheme, and in any case would have been far too frightened to have faced a board of men. To this day I can remember my utter astonishment when, on being asked if she felt I had any particular qualities, and would benefit from such a scholarship, this wee old-fashioned elderly teacher banged the desk with her clenched fist, sending the glasses rattling, and declared in an American idiom I never suspected she knew, 'I'd stake my bottom dollar on this girl.'

I trembled at the passion in her voice, and at her faith in me. 'What if I fail her?' I gasped to myself. 'What if she has to pay all the money back if I let her down?' I knew we hadn't a spare farthing to repay anybody, and I was sick with a sense of responsibility in case I ruined this new, violent Miss McKenzie.

As I've said, I was a natural swot, but even if I hadn't been, the memory of that indomitable little figure would have spurred me on when I felt like faltering.

At the end of my year at college I was able to lay before her the college gold medal as the year's top student, a bronze medal as a special prize in another subject, twenty pounds in prize money, and a whole sheaf of certificates.

And suddenly as I gazed at her, and saw her eyes sparkling with pride behind the gold-rimmed glasses, I realized how widely she had thrown open the door of opportunity for me. And I knew for the first time what the phrase 'entertaining angels unaware' meant. For there, standing before me in class, was my very own angel, Miss McKenzie.

But long before this, and before that visit to the theatre, when Shakespeare was revealed to me by real actors, one of the forms of our local entertainment which lured me like the candle to the moth was the annual kinderspiel put on by the Rechabites, a temperance society, commonly known as the Racky-bites. I joined this society purely and simply to get into the kinderspiel. Thoughts of temperance never entered into it, and one of my earliest attempts at being an entertainer took place at a Rechabite meeting. An important guest had failed to appear, and volunteers from the body of the hall were begged to step forward and provide the fun. I was about eight years old at the time and, swallowing nervously, but finding the call irresistible, I made my way to the platform and in a voice husky with emotion said I would dance the Highland Fling for them.

In full view of a highly diverted audience I first removed my tammy, then my coat, then a long string of 'amber' beads which were Grannie's and which hung to my waist, and might have banged back and forth as I danced, and lastly my cardigan. By this time the audience was convulsed. I was bewildered by their laughter, but quite undeterred. At last, having whetted their appetites with this innocent striptease, I plunged into my version of the Highland Fling, only narrowly avoiding leaping over the edge of the stage as I jerked forward a few dangerous paces with each step. Breathless and triumphant I finished to a round of warm applause and loud laughter. I then collected all my clothes and my beads and put them all on again to mounting cheers, before descending to make room for the next performer.

My appetite was well and truly aroused, and I was in a fever of impatience for the kinderspiel. I went to Wednesday rehearsals, fairly jumping with excitement and anticipation, and I deaved Grannie for weeks with every chorus in which it was to be my privilege to take part. I was to be an angel, one of a host of about thirty, and my eyes grew wide with joy as I thought of the white dress I would wear, the little white lacy shawl which would cover my curls and keep them dry *en route* from house to hall and, the most exotic final touch, of the sparkling glitter frost which would be sprinkled over the shawl to simulate glittering sequins or rain-drops, I wasn't sure which. I couldn't wait for the transformation which would turn me from a wee lassie in a jersey and a skirt to a beautiful white glittering 'angel'.

Then tragedy fell. Three weeks before the show, on the very night the artists' tickets were to be given out, I fell a victim of the virulent influenza bug. The tickets had to be handed to each child personally. The organizers were all busy working men, who gave their precious time to the Rechabites free of charge, and they point-blank refused to deal with requests other than at the fixed hour on that fixed night, and nobody could collect a ticket for anyone else. Flu or no, I was determined to get that ticket, but Grannie was adamant and paid scant heed to my bitter tears. 'You'll not step a foot outside this door the nicht,' she said. 'Do you want to get yer daith?' Death at that black moment seemed a simple punishment beside the anguish of missing the kinderspiel. But she was grown-up and I was small, and stay in bed I must.

I lay there, numb with despair, and then resilience flooded back. I knew what I would do. I would simply get better. I would get better more quickly than I had ever done before from previous flus, and I would get an artist's ticket if I had to steal one. So I did everything I was told without a murmur, and three days before the kinderspiel I was allowed out to play again.

Without a word to anybody, I stalked the organizer from his work to his house. We all knew where everybody in the district worked, and it was easy to wait for the half past five horn and follow him home. My heart was thumping, but my mind was fixed on that ticket. It was against all the rules, but I was past caring about that.

I knocked at the door. It was opened, and the organizer stood regarding me. 'Please,' I whispered, 'I was off when you gave out the tickets, and I'm an angel in the chorus, and I *must* be at the kinderspiel.' My eyes fixed on his imploringly. 'I've got my dress, and my sparkling frost and everything.' The last words shamed me by breaking on a half-sob. Suddenly the man smiled. 'I remember you,' he said amazingly. 'You're the wee lass who did the Highland Fling, aren't you?' I stared at him, speechless, and nodded. I had expected aloofness, argument, maybe instant refusal, but never in my wildest dreams recognition.

He looked at me thoughtfully for a moment. 'Would you like to do your Highland Fling again for us, but this time at the kinderspiel?' he asked. I gulped, visions of myself in my white dress and sparkling frost fading. 'But I'm an angel,' I said. A 'single' turn made no impression on my young mind. To be one of a band of angels was the summit of my ambition just then.

'Well, that's all right,' he said, 'you can still be an angel, but one of our dancers has fallen ill and we need something to fill that space, and your Highland Fling would be just the thing.'

'But what will I put on. I havenae got a kilt.' Although I didn't possess one myself, I well knew that all self-respecting Highland dancers wore kilts.

'You don't need a kilt,' he said surprisingly. 'Just you wear your wee jersey and skirt, and your long beads, and your cardigan and do it exactly as you did it before.' Something seemed to be amusing him, but I was in no mood to puzzle it out. The dazzling prospect of being at the kinderspiel at all was enough for me. When I ran home in triumph with the ticket Grannie said, 'Aye, I kent fine you'd get it, if you died in the attempt.' But she was smiling, not angry, although she had been aghast at hearing I'd followed the man home from his work.

There could never have been a happier angel than I

was on the night of the kinderspiel. Never was sparkling frost more liberally sprinkled, and never did leading lady feel more glamorous than I as I adjusted my woollie shawl over my hair and stepped proudly from the close on my way to the show. I was the only angel who had to change back into everyday clothes in the middle of the performance, and I sighed regretfully as I laid my heavenly garments aside for a brief space.

The lilt of the dance introduction was heard, and I went forward, feeling miserably conscious of my workaday attire. I did my innocent striptease, the forerunner of all stripteases I believe, and then went into my Highland Fling. It brought the house down, although the only one who couldn't understand the reason was me. When I solemnly raised my arms to remove the amber beads there was such a roar of laughter I nearly forgot the opening steps of the dance. I needed all my concentration to stay on the platform, for I've never been able to dance on the one spot, and this time as I surged wildly towards the edge, there was a yell of apprehension, then a gasp of relief as I stayed trembling on the very brink for the final step. I took the warning shouts for granted. They were just the yelps of my grannie as I staggered towards the fireplace at home, multiplied in several hundred throats. Their laughter was beyond me, but their concern quite understandable. 'Naebody would want to see a wee lassie falling over that terribly high platform,' I thought comfortably, as I panted to a triumphant conclusion, and, the cheers still ringing in my ears, I hurried backstage to put on my beautiful angel's dress again.

What did it matter to me that my unorthodox Highland Fling had been the hit of the evening? I was too young to realize what a happy fate it is to be able to make people laugh, and too excited to resent their laughing at my honest efforts.

I took my place, with bursting heart, among the angels once more and bounced out with most unholy glee, to yell out the closing chorus which said goodnight to our audience, and to the kinderspiel for that year.

Seven

One of the most dramatic stories told to me by my mother was of an accident to me in babyhood, when a tramcar was pressed into the rescue operation. I was about nine months old at the time and my mother had stood me up on the sink-ledge by the window while she cleared up the bathing things before putting me to bed.

The china bath, washed and dried, was beside me on the draining board, and when I turned round at the sound of my father's key in the door, my foot went through one handle, and I crashed to the floor. The bath broke into a dozen pieces, and an edge cut through the bridge of my nose like a knife. My mother used to shudder as she described the blood as 'spurting up like a well', but my father, quick as lightning, seized the two cut edges of my skin between his fingers, bade my mother throw a shawl round me, and before she knew what was happening had dashed down two flights of stairs, kicking over the basin of pipeclay water and the stair-woman in his flight. He leaped on to the driver's platform of a passing tramcar.

'Don't stop till you get to the Royal Infirmary,' he ordered. The driver was so impressed with his urgency that he did exactly that, and all the passengers were carried willy-nilly to the doors of the infirmary. To me the most impressive part of the story was that the tram wasn't even going near the infirmary on its route. It should have turned at right angles at the points long before then. I was astounded that a tramcar should have been used in this way as an ambulance for me, and that the driver had dared vary the route from that marked on the destination board.

It was maybe this thrilling piece of Weir folklore which started my love affair with tramcars. When I was a little girl I only had the penny for the homeward tram journey, when my legs were tired after the long walk into the town for special messages. It would have been impossibly extravagant to ride both ways. That luxury was only indulged in when travelling with Grannie, and the journey to town then seemed so different from the top deck of the tram, the landmarks so swiftly passed compared with my usual walking pace.

Later, when I went to college and the novelty of gazing out of the window had worn off, I used the travelling time to catch up on my studies. I'd be so absorbed in the intricacies of book-keeping, or French, or drama projects that only the changing note of the tram, and the memorized lurching motion as it neared my stop, warned me that I was home and it was time to get off.

I was amazed one day when a conductor said to me, 'I've watched you for years, and in all the time you've travelled on my car I've never seen you read a book just for pleasure – you're a great wee worker.' We knew all the conductors and conductresses by sight, of course, but the notion that they saw us as other than a hand holding out a fare was a great surprise.

The most sought-after seating was in the front section of the upstairs deck. This was a favourite meeting place for the youngsters, for it felt just like being on the bridge of a ship, and it was cut off by a door from the main top deck. We could sing or tell stories if we felt like it and were sure we were disturbing nobody. The driver, whom we'd forgotten, could hear every word, for we were sitting directly above his platform with only an open staircase between us. He didn't mind the singing at all, but if a foot-thumper kept up a steady drumming in time to the rhythm of the ditty he'd shout up to us to be quiet, or he'd come up and throw the lot of us off. This was enough to silence us, for it would have been a terrible waste to have been thrown off before the stage we'd paid for had been reached. We all loved riding in trams and quite often went right to the terminus to get our money's worth, and walked back the odd quarter-mile to our homes.

At one time fares weren't paid for in cash, but in little bone tokens which were bought in bulk at the tramway offices in town. I don't know why this precaution was taken, unless it made the conductor's bag lighter, or foiled a would-be thief, or a dishonest employee. Their colours fascinated me and I longed to save them up and use them at playing shops, but the tram rides they bought excited me even more, so I never possessed more than one at a time.

When I was very small the routes were indicated by the colour of the trams. When colours were replaced by numbers we thought we'd never get used to them. How could we be expected to remember the No 25 went to Springburn and Bishopbriggs when all our lives we'd travelled in a red car to our homes in these districts?

You could see colours a long way off, but you had to be fairly close to see a number, and the queues teetered uncertainly trying to decide which number suited them, and delayed the tram's departure. This infuriated the conductress, who would shout, 'Come on, youse. Whit are youse waitin' fur? The baund tae play?'

We could see no reason for this change, which confused us, unless the wild suggestion was true that it was because some people might be colour blind.

But we didn't resist for a single moment the arrival of the new tramcars. Such gleaming opulence, such luxurious chrome and glittering glass, such a richness of finish. We felt we were the envy of the entire country. We exclaimed over each splendid detail as though we had bought one privately. We used to wait for a new car, letting the shabby old faithfuls rattle past by the half-dozen, counting the time well spent to ride in such luxury.

This wasn't a habit indulged in by us alone. Some visiting relatives from America took me into town one day, and I heard the husband say to his wife that she must wait to travel in the newest tramcar, for they were the finest in the world. In the world! *We* thought they were, of course, but it was impressive to hear a visitor, and an American at that, agree with our opinion.

The new trams had a more sophisticated trolley arrangement than the old, so that hardly any skill or strength was required to swing it about for the return journey. With the older trams, the conductor had to exert some power and have a nice sense of accuracy to place the pulley against the overhead wire at the first attempt. We children used to cluster round the terminals, to assess the prowess of conductors, and we let them know in no uncertain terms just how good or bad they were.

Sometimes our mothers sent us to the terminus to get coppers for a sixpence, from the stock carried by the conductor. But, of course, if we'd been cheeky about his trolley attempts we could say goodbye to any thought of getting our money exchanged. There was nothing for it but to wait for the next tram, and stand admiringly by, hoping our compliments on the trolley finesse would soften the conductor and we'd get our coppers.

When the old cars were moving, these trolleys could be temperamental, especially if the driver was new. There would be a lurch, and the trolley would come bouncing off the overhead wire in a shower of sparks, and swing wildly back and forth as the car slithered to a halt. This was a nerve-racking experience for the timid, and there would be shouts, 'The trolley's off – the trolley's off', and all eyes would fasten anxiously on the conductor as he swung it towards the overhead wire again.

There was no danger, but it made us all uneasy to feel we were sitting there unconnected to that magic overhead wire. If this happened three or four times in the course of a journey, there would be alarmed tut-tutting from the women, and contemptuous opinions from the men that the driver had 'nae idea how to drive a caur'. 'Aye, he must be new,' somebody would murmur. 'He juist hasnae got the hang o' it.' Even with trams there were plenty of back-seat drivers.

When a ha'penny was laid on the tramlines it became a pretended penny after the tram had thundered over it and flattened it out most satisfactorily. To achieve this, we flirted under the wheels of the trams quite fearlessly, for we were so familiar with the sight of them rocketing past our windows we saw little danger. I never knew any child to be injured by a tram. We were as sure-footed as mountain deer, and the drivers were quick to spot a faltering childish stumble on the rare occasion this happened, and to apply the brakes in good time. They'd all played on the tramlines themselves when children, and our games didn't make them turn a hair. If a child was occasionally scooped up in the 'cow-catcher' – a metal shovel arrangement worked by the driver to remove any obstacle in his path – well, that was all right. Wasn't that what the cow-catcher was

there for? And it would be a good lesson to the young-
ster for the future.

But if we treated the dangers of being run down by
a tramcar with contempt, there were plenty of other
fears which shook us by the throat in our tenement
games. There was the mysterious creature called 'Flannel Feet'. Nobody had ever actually seen him, but his
nameless exploits filled us with such dread that it was a
brave child who would go up a strange close in the
dark. Even on our own familiar stair landings, a broken
light would send us scurrying past the dark corners
with pounding hearts, sure that this terrifying Flannel
Feet would be lurking in the shadows. The fact that we
never knew a single person who'd been attacked meant
nothing. We frightened each other with stories which
came from nowhere. A childish game called 'Robinson
Crusoe' was the source of such a tale. In this game
somebody had to hide, and we others rushed about,
calling up closes and in alley-ways, with our hands
cupped to our mouths to send our voices soaring:

> Robinson Crusoe give us a call,
> Give us an answer or nothing at all.

The one hiding would call out in a high disguised voice
'Pee-wee' and we'd try to guess the direction of the
sound and set off in pursuit. Then the victor would
hide. Frightening tales were told of the answering 'Pee-
wee' having been given by Flannel Feet, when the

unsuspecting searcher fell straight into his clutches. Strangely enough, we never even asked for details of what this monster *did*. His mere existence brought terror to us.

The cemetery was another source of shivering fright. To pass its wall on a dark night was a dare few of us accepted, for didn't we all know ghosts gathered behind the wall, ready to pounce on the unwary? Sometimes in winter, made brave by numbers after our slides on the ice, we'd perch on this wall and sing, 'I am a poor wee orphan, my mother she is dead', our eyes darting to the tombstones beyond. But one verse was enough, and we'd slither down, and race for home, glad to have escaped the clutch of ghostly fingers.

Living in our own world, as we children did, it never occurred to us that grown-ups could ever be nervous or frightened. We knew mothers and grannies were brave and strong, and weren't even afraid of the dark. You couldn't even scare them by jumping round a corner unexpectedly, and the last thing I dreamed of was that I, a particularly nervous wee creature, could instil real fear into anyone, least of all my beloved grannie. And yet I did it, all unknowingly, one terrible winter afternoon.

Grannie had slipped downstairs to visit a neighbour while we were at school, and when I came in at four o'clock I found the door 'off the sneck', and pushed it open. I was so entranced at the cosy warmth of the firelight that instead of going in search of her as I usually did, I curled up in the armchair to wait quietly till she came in to light the gas and maybe make a cup of tea. I was strictly forbidden to light the gas mantle anyway, which was out of reach unless I stood on a chair.

It grew darker and darker, and at last I heard Grannie's light footstep and the rustle of her long skirt as she pushed the door open. For some reason, which I can't explain to this day, instead of calling out, 'Is that you, Grannie?', I sat completely silent. She picked up the matches from the dresser, moved towards the gas mantle, and then stopped with a frightened intake of breath, sensing somebody was in the kitchen. By this time, the whole situation was so unreal. I was too scared to open my mouth. Grannie's eyes searched the shadows, picking up the outline of a body in the chair, but instead of recognizing me, she gave a strangled cry, dropped the matches and rushed towards the door.

Now, thoroughly frightened at the effect I'd had on her, and terrified of retribution, I called out in a hysterical giggle, 'Grannie, it's me.' She stopped as if she had been shot, and turned back. 'You!' she cried, in such a tone of horror at my wickedness that I burst into tears. 'Why didn't you speak when I came in?' she demanded. 'I might have had a heart attack. Fancy thinking out such a cruel thing to do to your grannie.'

She sat down, trembling, too shocked even to light the gas.

I was in such a turmoil of confusion it was like a bad dream. Why had I done it? I didn't know. But fancy my brave grannie being frightened of me? Rushing to make amends, I leaped on a chair, seized a small glass from the shelf and poured a tot of our medicinal whisky into it and urged Grannie to drink it to steady her nerves. I'd seen my mother do this when a neighbour's little girl was run over by a push-bike, and it had magic properties then, and it would surely help Grannie at this moment. Grannie took one sip and let out a yell that scared me half out of my wits. In the dark I hadn't noticed that there was a sewing needle in the glass, put there out of harm's way, and Grannie had nearly swallowed it. Was there no end to the damage I was capable of on this black afternoon?

My mother, of course, was told of the whole wicked episode when she came in from work, and I was duly punished. As I lay crying in bed, I was bewildered and tried to understand how it had all happened. It seemed to me it all started because Grannie had been frightened by a shadow which she didn't know was me. I hadn't known till then that grown-ups could fear the unknown just as we children feared the invisible Flannel Feet. And for the first time I began to wonder if maybe even Flannel Feet wasn't a bogey-man at all, but just somebody like me who should have had the sense to open his mouth and speak, instead of creating an atmosphere of terror merely by keeping quiet at the wrong time.

But if we children hadn't actually met a bogey-man we knew everybody else within a radius of a quarter of a mile of our tenements. A stranger trying to lure any of us would have had a thin time. We knew the habits, good and bad, of the entire adult community. Our mothers and grannies saw no sense in hiding from us the evil effects of drink, and we saw enough drunkenness to make us teetotallers for life. We saw with horror how drink could turn a quiet father into a wild creature who could beat up his wife, and we saw ashamed women taking bundles to the pawn on Monday mornings to raise enough cash to carry them through the week, because earnings had been swallowed in weekend drinking.

With the harsh judgement of children we saw them all in black and white. Mr Grant was avoided because he drank. We'd *seen* him on Saturday nights, so it was no good telling us he might be as docile as a lamb during the rest of the week, and maybe even a better husband and father than somebody else whose sins weren't so obvious and which we wouldn't have understood.

A puzzling figure in this assessment was that of Mr Carr. He was an old soldier, carried himself straight as a ramrod, and always looked, in my mother's words, 'as if he came out of a band-box'. Yet, according to my grannie, 'he drank like a fish'. How could Grannie, and other people too, say such a thing when I'd never seen him drunk? 'Aye ye widnae, lassie,' said old Mrs Peebles, his mother-in-law, when I asked her. 'He carries it weel, I'll say that, but he drinks away every penny just the same.' I knew she was a God-fearing truthful old lady, who was always reading her Bible when I went in to see if she wanted any messages, so I believed her; and Mr Carr joined the ranks of those who must be avoided, especially on Saturday nights.

And yet it was Mr Carr who taught me that there are many shades between black and white, and maybe even streaks of pure gold where they were least expected.

My brothers had been playing piggy-back on the staircase on the way up to our second-storey house, and when they reached our door the younger one had fallen with a terrible crash and hit his head on the sharp edge of the stair-rise. Grannie had no need to scold, for that still figure had quenched all argument on the part of my brother. By the time I arrived home from school, the doctor was busy at the bedside and my mother had been sent for from work. 'Severe concussion' was the verdict and my mother and Grannie were instructed what to do. Bottles of medicine were ranged along the dresser, but against all of them the small patient, with clenched teeth, rebelled and refused to swallow a drop. It had been impressed on us that the 'opening' medicine was vital, but, ill as he was, nothing would make the rebel swallow it. We tried everything. Even giving it to him as though he were a puppy, and holding his lips until he appeared to swallow. The minute the hand was taken away, he spat it up, or threw it up, and this seemed to go on for days.

I think everybody knew of our difficulties except the doctor. For some reason my mother and Grannie were frightened to admit no medicine had been swallowed, in case the wee chap would be removed to hospital. We had a terror of hospitals in the tenements, as so many who went there never seemed to come back. Or it could have been we just couldn't afford the fee for another visit from the doctor.

With the complete involvement of tenement neighbours, everybody on the stair and nearby had weighed in with ideas and suggestions. Old quarrels were forgotten as each rushed in with what seemed the perfect solution. No good. The patient grew more limp and exhausted, and we were desperate. It was Saturday night. My brother was afraid of only two things. Drunks and soldiers. In despair, my mother moved to the window, biting her lip to stop the tears, when suddenly she saw the upright figure of Mr Carr passing the close. She threw up the window, 'Mr Carr,' she called down, 'wait a minute. Can I speak to you?' I was horrified. Didn't my mother know he would be on his way to the pub to drink like a fish? How could a drunk man help us?

But my mother was inspired. She'd remembered my brother's fear. She'd remembered too that Mr Carr kept his sergeant's uniform well pressed for his Territorial meetings. Hadn't she always said he looked as if he'd come out of a band-box. She knew it was Saturday all right. But she also knew in our tenement world everybody shared the griefs and worries of the other, and it was certain Mr Carr, who only lived round the corner and whose mother-in-law often visited Grannie, was aware of the drama which had been going on with the small patient.

With zest he entered into the conspiracy. The pub was forgotten. Quickly he changed into his awe-inspiring uniform, and with cane under his arm, and peaked cap down on his nose, he thundered at the door. 'Where's this rebellious boy?' he demanded. 'Give me the medicine,' and he held out an imperious hand. My brother's lips parted in terror. The spoon was inserted. The medicine went down. 'Now,' said Mr Carr in a voice which shook the ornaments on the shelf, 'if you don't *keep* it down, you'll be sentenced to fourteen days in the guardroom.' Nobody knew what that meant, but it sounded terrible. Terrible enough for the patient to keep his lips tightly closed. Next day the medicine had done its work. From that moment my brother started on the long slow road to recovery. It was a miracle. But the greatest miracle, it seemed to me, was that we owed it all to a man who could drink like a fish. I never forgot Mr Carr. And, apart maybe from Hitler, from that day I never believed anyone was entirely bad.

In spite of Grannie's wizardry with cheap cuts of meat, and marrow bones, and food which would 'stick to wur ribs', as Grannie would say, there always seemed to be a space in our tummies which was never quite filled. And in summer-time one of the very nicest ways of trying to fill this space when we had a ha'penny to spare was at the Tallies. I don't suppose any of us suspected we were abbreviating the word 'Italians', as we raced from school to the Tallies in search of one of the many wonders within its small interior. At that time all the ice-cream in Glasgow seemed to be made by Italians. And I don't even suppose the lazily good-tempered proprietrix minded being called a Tallie. She knew we loved her. She knew we were dazzled with admiration of the splendid marble counter, the glittering mirrors which lined the walls, the little round marble-topped tables, the neat chairs, all so different from the wooden fixtures in the old-fashioned shops which were her neighbours.

Her broken English was a constant fascination to our ears, and her unruly mop of crinkly black hair and brandy-ball brown eyes two more exotic signs that she came from a faraway country. Before I was big enough to toddle down to buy anything, the bigger girls would take me with them, and the large-hearted Tallie would lift me up on to the counter and break off pieces of thick slab chocolate from an open packet she'd been nibbling, and pop them into my all-too-willing mouth. I'd have to sing her a wee song afterwards, in payment, and of course I was certain I was getting the biggest bargain in Glasgow. She was never too busy to play this game. She was very fond of a wee poem too, which seemed to amuse her, coming from a two-year-old like me. It went:

> A house to let, apply within.
> A lady put out for drinking gin.
> Gin you know is a very bad thing.
> A house to let, apply within.

I could almost measure my growing up against my purchases at the Tallies. When I was very small a ha'penny cone not much fatter than my thumb was as much as I could manage. Then, as I grew bigger and was able to earn some pocket money running messages, for the neighbours of course – I didn't get money for running our own messages – I moved on to penny cones, tuppeny wafers, threepenny sponges, single nougats, sugar wafers and, beyond these, oh unbeliev-able splendour, to such wondrous delights as a 98, which was a double sponge filled with ice-cream and a half-bar of cream chocolate. The first time my teeth plunged into this delicacy and met first sponge, then the chill of ice-cream, then the strange flavour of cold chocolate and its creamy centre, I thought experience could go no further.

In winter we didn't eat ice-cream at all. It was purely a summer delight. I had an aunt who was regarded as quite eccentric because she continued to indulge her passion for ice-cream beyond the summer season. She used to send us down for fourpence-worth in a jug, in the depths of winter, and we watched her curiously as she ate it, but refused to touch a spoonful ourselves, for there was something about wintry blasts and ice-cream which offended our sense of correctness.

In winter, our Tallie went over to hot peas, and no peas cooked at home ever tasted half as good as those bought in that wee shop. A penny bought a cup of 'pea brae', which was actually the thickened water in which the peas had been boiled, liberally seasoned with pepper and a good dash of vinegar. There was always the excitement of maybe finding a few squashed peas at the bottom of the cup, and we would feel about with our spoon, eyes lighting with joy if we found something solid and knew we had struck gold. How we dallied over each spoonful so that we could enjoy the warmth and camaraderie of the clean little shop as long as possible, for now it was cosy and heated, and steaming with cooking peas. The lordly ones seated at the tables consumed threepenny plates of peas, which made us sick with envy, but when the day arrived when we were big enough and rich enough to spend threepence in one go, I found to my surprise and disappointment that I preferred the penny 'pea brae'.

Alas, I lost my taste for hot peas and vinegar altogether the night I took scarlet fever, for I'd eaten this dish earlier in the evening, and the first sign that all was not well with me was the irritation the vinegar caused to my tender throat. Ever afterwards scarlet fever and hot peas were synonymous to me.

But before this disaster struck, that same aunt of the ice-cream orgies would occasionally take a fancy for peas. I was delighted when she'd send me down for sixpence-worth in the jug. Grannie snorted contemptuously at this extravagance. 'H'm, paying good money to get somebody else to do your cooking for you,' she'd say to my aunt, 'and peas biled awa' to nothing at that.' But that was precisely what our depraved tastes enjoyed, and there was a sort of wild indulgence in buying cooked food. We would sit round the fire, the sixpence-worth of peas divided out into saucers, the pepper and vinegar duly added, and our delightful, eccentric aunt would teach me to sing with her in harmony, in between sips and chewing of peas. There we would sit, singing soulfully 'Let the rest of the world go by', and she would make me switch from melody to harmony to make sure I knew what I was doing, until my brothers grew fed up and demanded to be told some jokes, and the evenings would end in a riot of laughter.

But Grannie didn't always object to buying food cooked by other folk, especially when it was fish and chips. Tenement families hadn't the space or the money to keep a pan of fat for deep frying, and that was where the chip-shops came into their own. They played a tremendously important part in our lives.

There were four fish-and-chip shops within ten minutes' walking distance of our house (or six minutes if we ran, as we usually did). Each had a subtle advantage over the others, which made choice agonizing when one's mother forgot to say which shop was to be patronized.

If it was your own pocket money, of course, the choice of shop was dictated by the amount of cash in hand. When it was a ha'penny, Jimmy's was the only possible choice, for he alone understood infant economics, and he saved all the wee hard bits of potato which floated to the top of the fryer, and kept them in a separate partition, hot, crisp and greasy, ready to be served out by the fistful at a ha'penny a time, when we hungrily demanded, 'Ony crimps, Jimmy?' We were allowed to salt them, but no vinegar was provided. As he reasonably pointed out, he couldn't make any profit at all if he supplied vinegar on ha'penny sales, an argument which we felt was quite sound.

A penny in our pockets saw us deserting generous Jimmy for the shop at the bend of the road, where the marble counter reached to our noses, and where they sold the most mouth-watering potato fritters for three a penny. What pleasure to crunch through the thin layer of batter and reach the steaming potato in the centre.

When we had the rich sum of tuppence we went round the corner to the shop where they sold pies and black puddings. We had no intention of buying such delicacies ourselves – tuppence wouldn't have stretched so far – but we went for the sheer thrill of listening to the plutocrats who *could* order such foods, and for the pleasure we derived from watching the assistant lower pie or pudding into the hot fat. We admired his judgement in knowing the exact moment to whisk out pie or pudding, glistening and rich with fat. Sometimes a purchaser would grandly demand tuppence-worth of pickles to enhance the feast, and we gazed at each other with smiles of delight that we were in the presence of such extravagant living.

Across the road and round the far corner was the fourth shop, to which our mothers sent us when we could coax them to buy chips for supper. 'Very clean,' my mother would say, 'everything spotless.' We weren't all that impressed with this praise, because the bags in which the chips were daintily shovelled were scandalously small, but we daren't disobey and go where the helpings were bigger, because at that time this was the only shop using those wee bags.

Quality as opposed to quantity was an unknown factor in our voracious young lives, and we didn't trouble to hide our feelings as we watched the assistant blow out the diminutive bag in readiness for the disgustingly small helpings of chips. 'Humph!' we'd mutter audibly. 'Hauds practically nane! Some profit they must be makin'.' At that the assistant would fix us with steely blue eye and say, 'I've a good mind tae take aff a few, just fur yer cheek!' 'Aw don't dae that, Jessie,' we'd cry in anguish, 'we were just kiddin' ye. Pit oan a wee tait mair, go'n, Jessie, some fell aff yer shovel when ye were liftin' them oot.' And because she was a good sort she would toss in maybe half a dozen on top of the bag, and we'd sneak out a couple on the way home, for, after all, they were a sort of bonus.

We didn't often have fish from these shops, for my mother's tightly stretched budget just wouldn't stretch to such extravagance. But on gala nights, such as when she was indulging her weakness for flitting, as she did five times in two years, my mother would acknowledge that willing helpers had to be fed after their labours, and there could only be one choice for the feast – fish and chips.

As the last piece of furniture was being dragged round the bend of the stair, and the helpers (all pals of my brothers and myself) panted and puffed to get it into the house unscathed, I was sent to the best chip-shop for three or four fish suppers, and an extra sixpence-worth of chips. This was a far cry from a ha'penny-worth of crimps at Jimmy's, and I hoped as many of my chums as possible would be there to hear me place this staggering order. This rich feast was wrapped in several thicknesses of newspaper to keep the grease from going through to my jersey, and I ran like the wind back to the new abode, hugging my steaming bundle to my bosom, to deliver it as hot as possible to the weary workers. When I arrived the party would be sitting round the freshly laid table, clean, and flushed with anticipation, empty plates in front of each. My mother carefully divided out the portions – the biggest helpings going to the biggest lads, for they'd done the heaviest work, right down to the smallest person in the house who had only run round with small items like shovels and brushes.

Piles of bread and butter and margarine and lashings of tea were provided, and our voices rose happily as the crisp batter and the golden chips disappeared down hungry throats.

Weirs' flittings were much sought-after social occasions among our crowd, for the fish and chip feast which ended the evening's labours was a golden bait which drew more volunteers than we could use.

These flittings were a miracle of neighbourly assistance and organization, for the only item which cost money was the horse and cart, and even that was only hired if the distance was just too far for the helpers to walk. They all took place after the day's work, for nobody dreamed of taking time off just to move house. After a quick tea, pals and neighbours rolled up, dressed in dungarees or peenies, and the tasks were handed out according to ability or nimbleness. The children ran about like ants with the small items from the fireplace, clearing the place so that the men could move the furniture more easily. Advice was shouted as tricky bends of the stair were negotiated. 'Aye, a wee bit your wey, Wullie, that's it!', or 'Naw, naw, you'll hiv to go back – you're too tight roon' this corner, ye'll never dae it'. My mother's heart would be in her mouth during these operations, in case her precious wardrobe would get scratched, but these men were no amateurs. They'd helped at dozens of flittings and the furniture was in good hands. Meanwhile, another expert would be prising the linoleum up, and rolling it carefully so that it wouldn't crack. 'Aye,' my mother would say with satisfaction, 'that's the best of real inlaid linoleum, you can lift it and lay it a dizzen times and never a crack in it!' Willing hands were taking the big brass covers off the wall and wrapping them in newspapers, and piling them into an empty clothes basket, and other hands raced downstairs with it when it was full, tucked the covers safely beside the bedding, and raced back again with the empty basket, to have it filled again with the precious china, or 'cheenie' as everybody in our tenements called it. This was the women's work, and most tenderly each piece was wrapped in newspaper, and instructions called out to the couriers, 'Noo mind ye pit it a' on something soft, so that it'll no' shoogle in the kert. Pit the pillows roon' it noo, Jimmy, so it'll no' break.'

At the other end, another small army was waiting to unload the lorry, and everything sat on the pavement until the linoleum was re-laid in the new house, then more frantic activity to put everything in its new setting. How different everything looked, even if we'd only moved to the next close, which my mother did twice, for we knew our houses so intimately that the slightest variation in a lobby or a window frame, or the size of a fireplace, was of enormous significance. Everybody loved a flitting. Nobody minded the hard work. It was all fun, a real diversion, and it always ended up with a party, and who cared if it also ended up with an empty purse?

Eight

But however willingly shoulders were put to the wheel when they were needed, we weren't angels, and there were plenty of rows to whip up passions and cause the tongues to cluck in fury or sympathy. We lived so close to one another in the tenements, it would have been a wonder if there had been no clash of personalities, no misunderstandings which led to feuds which could last for weeks, until a common bond of suffering or hardship drew the rival factions together again.

One such feud went on for nearly six weeks between Mrs MacFarlane and Mrs Brown. The husbands didn't enter into it, and, ignoring their wives' temperaments, went on nodding to one another when they met as though they'd never heard of the word 'feud'. The two women had fallen out over an argument as to whose turn it was for the washing-house key, and Mrs MacFarlane would pass Mrs Brown with lowered eyes, without a word of greeting. Their children were greatly irritated by this state of affairs. Their social system of bartering was ruined, and they found it maddening not to be able to exchange puzzles or 'bools' with each other, just because their mothers weren't on speaking terms.

Then one day of heart-stopping drama there was a

squeal of brakes, and the cow-catcher of a tram swiftly and neatly scooped up little Annie Brown, who had fallen right across the path of the tram as she tried to retrieve her ball. Her mother had seen the whole thing from her top-floor kitchen window where she was performing her toilet. In her fright she dashed down and into the street, wearing no more than a camisole and skirt, to find that Mrs MacFarlane, her feuding neighbour, had already taken wee Annie into her house and was gently crooning and comforting the sobbing child. The whole street found the reunion most impressive, but almost greater than the relief that things were back to normal was our shocked amazement that Mrs Brown hadn't even realized she had been standing there in the middle of the main road in her camisole! Half-naked, for all to see!

Our own feud started when the neighbours across the landing acquired an Airedale dog. This beast had only to see a child and the staircase would echo with its furious barking and snarling, and the sight of its lip drawn back from long sharp teeth filled me with terror. It was no good Grannie telling me a barking dog couldn't bite at the same time. I didn't intend to give it the chance, and I'd run like the wind past their open door.

Neighbourly relations were undisturbed nevertheless, until the night I was sent down to the local fish-shop for fish and chips, a great treat which was provided by a visiting auntie. As I reached our landing, the Airedale, scenting the delicious aroma leaped at me.

In spite of my terror, I clung to the precious parcel, but my screams opened every door on the stair. There was a furious row, for fright made me so sick that I couldn't touch food that night, or all next day, and Grannie had told Mrs Petrie, the dog's owner, that she would report her to the factor of the property for keeping a dangerous animal.

This was *far* worse than the wash-house-key rows. To be reported to the factor was as bad as being reported to the police. Worse, in fact, for the factor could turn you out of your house and could certainly make anyone get rid of a dangerous dog.

No word was exchanged between the families as they passed each other on the stair. The Petries' door was kept closed at all times, so the Airedale was heard but not seen, thank goodness.

When it was their turn for the washing-house the key was slipped through their letter-box, not handed over as was usually the case. When it came round to paying their share for washing the staircase window their few pence were wrapped in a twist of paper and put through our letter-box. Goodness knows how long this feud would have lasted, but I took a very bad dose of gastric flu, and my appetite vanished completely for nearly a fortnight. Grannie and my mother tried to tempt me with everything within their modest means, but listlessly I refused the lot. I grew thinner and whiter and they were at their wits' end. Then one day a delicious smell of chicken broth drifted across the landing. We all knew the Petries were quite well off, for weren't they all out working, with four pay-packets coming into the house? We only saw chicken soup at Christmas, and not always then, so my passion for it could only be satisfied once a year at the very most. When Grannie came over to the bed to ask, 'What would you like to eat?', I whispered, 'Some of Mrs Petrie's soup.'

Grannie stared at me. She was a marvellous cook, and at any other time would have felt outraged to go to anybody and confess I fancied something I couldn't find in her cooking. But now it was the first food I'd fancied for two whole weeks. And yet they weren't on speaking terms. It was impossible. My mother, who was in from her work for lunch, said, 'I'll go. I'll ask.'

Bravely she knocked at the Petries' door. She was met by an icy glare, and a dry 'Yes, Mrs Weir? What is it?'

My mother swallowed her pride. She explained how ill I'd been. That I'd eaten nothing sustaining for a fortnight, but today had smelt Mrs Petrie's soup, and if only she could spare a bowlful it might start my recovery. My mother told us later that Mrs Petrie's face broke into a smile as if she'd come into a fortune. In our poor community about the only thing anyone could afford to give away was a share of their food. But to be asked for soup by her feuding neighbour, when Grannie was herself known for her fine cooking, was the perfect compliment, and a sweet revenge.

Mrs Petrie brought in the bowl with her own hands, and watched me sup every drop of her fine soup. Later she claimed, 'It was my soup that saved Molly Weir's life.' We didn't argue about that exaggerated interpretation of the situation. We felt we had truly exchanged a feud for a mess of potage.

And we felt *our* feud had been on a far more dramatic scale than the usual petty squabbles over washing-house keys. The wash-house was in the back court, and each one served the twelve families in each tenement close, so a strict rota system operated for all the days of the week. As nobody wanted to wash at the weekends, each person's turn came round every twelve days. Domestic circumstances often led to the mothers swopping days with each other, and that was where the trouble started. If Mrs Brown swopped Tuesday for Thursday, then the woman who was entitled to the key after Mrs Brown had to be alerted, so *she* would know from whom to expect the key. But sometimes the woman who normally followed the exchanged day pretended she was entitled to the key following the swop day, and that was when the arguments started. With the meagre wardrobes we all possessed it must have been a nightmare trying to keep families in clean and dry clothes for twelve days between washing days, so an earlier washday was a blessing, and a wet day a tragedy. One couldn't blame them for trying a bit of cheating to get the key ahead of their turn.

There was never the same fierce competition to use the wash-house at night as there was in the daytime. Some of the night washers were younger women, daughters of those too old to do their washing during the day. They had the time, those elderly mothers, but not the strength, so the daughters had to tackle the household washing when they'd finished their day's work in shop or factory. Other women preferred to do their washing in the evenings for their own private reasons. My mother tut-tutted over this, for she felt washings ought properly to be done during the day when there was some chance of clothes being hung out in the fresh air and the wind, to dry, and acquire a fine fresh smell. Grannie would purse her lips and shake her head at the thought of pulleys in the kitchen, laden with steaming clothes, flapping in folks' faces as they moved back and forward to get the kettle from the range or put some coal on the fire. 'I don't like a hoose fu' o' wet cloots,' she'd say. 'It canna be good for thae lassies efter bein' oot at their work a' day.'

My mother would say of a neighbour who could easily have done the washing during the day, 'Aye, she must be awfu' glad to get away from her man and her weans when she'd put up with the damp cold of that wash-house instead of sitting at her own fireside.' And then she'd soften when Grannie would reply, 'Och well, maybe she's better off at that, for her man's a surly blackguard and gey poor company.'

Grannie's use of the word blackguard, which she pronounced 'blaggard', always sent a shiver down my spine, and I thought she'd invented this damning description herself. I was astounded in later years when

I came across the word again and again to describe the villains in the romances I devoured, and realized that Grannie's blackguard was a well-known character to many authors.

Far from sharing my mother's condemnation of the night washers, I used passionately to hope I could coax her to become one of them. There was a theatrical air about the whole scene which made a great appeal to me. The ordinary grey-stone wash-house of the day-time was transformed, as though at the wave of a magic wand, and I couldn't imagine that I had ever played shops on its window-ledge, or jumped from its roof on to the wall which divided the back courts.

Guttering candles, stuck in the necks of bottles and ranged along the window-sill, provided the only illumination in what now seemed a vast cavern. Mysterious shadows flickered in the far corners, and the foaming suds in the tubs took on a romantic radiance. When the lid of the huge brick boiler was raised to see how the 'white things' were progressing (the 'white things' was our name for all the household linen), swirling steam filled the wash-house, the candles spat and flickered through illuminated clouds, and the scene became fearsome as pictures of hell. The washerwoman bending over her tub changed from her everyday self too. Hair curled round her ears with the damp, cheeks flushed with the heat and the work, and eyes glowed in the candlelight, and she revealed a beauty I'd never noticed before.

Like animals attracted by the light, other women would drift from their tenements into the back court, and pause at the wash-house door. 'Are you nearly done noo?' was the usual greeting. The patient figure at the tubs, or 'bines' as we called them, would pause from her vigorous rubbing of the soiled clothes against the wash-board, charmed to be the centre of interest for once, and say cheerfully, 'Just aboot half-way through. I've juist the dungarees to dae, and then the white things will be ready for "sihnin" oot.' I once asked my teacher how to spell this word 'sihnin' which we used when we meant rinsing, but she'd never heard of it, for she was from the north, so I just had to make a guess at the spelling and hope I was right.

At the word 'dungarees' the women would groan in sympathy. Washing dungarees was a job they all hated, and as ours was a Railway district, most husbands or brothers or sons worked with dirty machinery, and came home with grease-laden dungarees, so this was a task they all had to face. Our tenement women all had raw fingers from using the slimy black soap and soda which was the only way they knew for ridding the filthy overalls of their accumulated grease and workshop dirt.

The women's eyes would lazily follow the washer's movements as she scrubbed and rinsed, and put clothes through the wringer ready for the house pulleys, or maybe for the ropes next morning, if the next woman using the wash-house could be coaxed to let her put out a rope for a couple of hours before her own were ready to be hung out. But the ropes were only put outside if it promised to be a fine day, and the women were expert weather forecasters, for everybody detested getting their nicely wrung clothes wet again. The ultimate in disaster was reached when the weight of sodden clothes on the ropes was too much for the supporting clothes poles, and the whole lot came crashing among the dirt of the back court, and had to be taken in and rinsed through all over again.

I loved when the white things were judged to be ready, for then came the scene I liked best of all. The heavy boiler lid was lifted right off, and leaned carefully against the back wall of the wash-house. Clouds of steam rushed everywhere. Up the chimney, out of the open door, into every corner. The washer, a long pole held in both hands, bent over the seething mass in the boiler, fished out a load, expertly twirling the steaming clothes to keep them safely balanced, and then ran with the laden pole across to the tub of clean water. Quickly and neatly a twist of the pole shot the clothes into the rinsing water. Back and forth, back and forth she went, her figure ghost-like in the rushing steam, until the boiler was empty. I longed to be allowed to help in this exciting operation, but met with scandalized refusal. 'Do you want to burn yoursel' to the bone?' the washerwoman would say in answer to my coaxing. 'You'll have this job to dae soon enough, hen, and then you'll no' be so pleased. Run away hame to your bed, or

I'll tell your grannie on you!' But the women were more amused than angry at my interest in their activities, and they made sure I went nowhere near the steam.

When this final rinsing stage was reached the watching women lingering at the doors couldn't resist a bit of advice, especially if the washer was a younger unmarried woman. As the tub filled, they'd say, 'Take oot the plug, hen, and let the clean water run through the claes. You'll get rid o' a' the soap faur quicker that way.' Or, 'Jessie, you're just squeezin' the soap into them again – you'll ha'e tae gi'e them another water. You're putting them through the wringer too soon.'

They were all experts. This was their world. And the young washerwoman would listen to them all, glad of their company and of their advice, for it was a great source of pride to have someone say, 'Aye, she hangs out a lovely washing.' And the most disparaging thing a tenement woman could say of another's wash-house efforts were the damning words, 'She's hangin' oot her *grey* things!'

Another glimpse of the world of washing day could be caught at the 'steamy', when we went to the baths. These were tubs and apparatus hired by women who had no proper wash-house in their tenement back courts, or who preferred the community atmosphere of the 'steamy' to a solitary session in their own wash-house. I used to pause in the open doorway, on my way out to the street, and watch the women at their work. It was like a scene from a play. The rising clouds of steam, the bare arms rhythmically rising and falling, the stately tread to the drying cupboards, and the measured walk back, bearing their washing gracefully before them, ready for packing into their prams or bogies for the homeward journey. Again I had a great longing to penetrate these mysteries and take part in the ritual myself, but I never did so, and these tantalizing glimpses were all I ever knew of this enchanting side of the baths.

When we children spoke of 'the baths' we meant the swimming pond, of course. Tuesdays were reserved for the girls, the other days for the boys, which seemed a bit unfair, but it was generally conceded that the boys seemed to enjoy the baths more than we did, and used them much oftener. We were quite happy, really, with our Tuesdays, and felt very privileged as we hurried up the road to make the most of 'our' day.

In summer, during school holidays, we met in the back court at half past seven in the morning, armed with our 'chittering bites'. Goodness knows how this habit arose, for nobody particularly liked early rising, but, once out of our cosy beds, there was something exciting and different about walking up Springburn Road when the streets were clean and quiet, and when the air had an unaccustomed freshness.

Some of the more opulent girls, who actually went to the seaside every summer, possessed their own bathing suits, but most of us hired a suit for a penny. The 'costumes', as we called them, were all the same size, and it depended on the size of the wearer whether the costume was short or long, tight or floppy. As one of the smallest girls in the neighbourhood, mine was held up in front by two huge safety pins on each shoulder, but even so the plunging neckline was all too revealing of my narrow chest, and the legs hung down unfashionably over my knees. But who cared? The laughter and derisive comments were all part of the fun. I had coaxed Grannie to buy me a natty black and white check rubber cap to protect my curls, and this sign of class earned me the greatest respect from my chums, and quenched their laughter over my floppy costume. *Their* caps were mere helmet affairs which pressed ears tightly to scalp and almost completely deafened them, but mine had elastic round the edge and gave me the tremendous advantage, I thought, of missing *nothing* of the yelling and joyous joking which was the non-stop accompaniment of our visits to the baths.

Once stripped, some would jump in recklessly from the side of the pond without even testing the water with an exploratory toe. Others cautiously descended the three or four steps at the shallow end and then gently lowered themselves into the water. A few compromised, and stood on the top step at the shallow end and 'scooshed' forward, with tremendous squealing from everyone in their path as the water drenched them.

There were rings suspended from the ceiling on long ropes, from which we would swing like monkeys, high over the water. It was a great dare to use the rings over the deep end of the pond, for if the arms tired and we were forced to drop into the water, we'd have to be dragged gasping to the side by one of the bigger girls. Only a few could dive, and the rest would gaze awestruck as some large girl self-consciously mounted the dale (our name for the high diving board) and stood poised, before leaping down in what, to us, was a magnificent dive and an inspiring deed of courage.

When we decided we had had enough of our water frolics, i.e., when our lips were blue with cold, what bliss to return to our boxes and scrub our shivering bodies with the hard towel we had been given with our entrance ticket, and to plunge chattering teeth into the crisp butteriness of the roll we'd brought with us as our 'chittering bite'. Nothing ever tasted quite so delicious as that roll, eaten in that particular atmosphere, and never was undervest so comforting to the skin as the one pulled over our heads in the dank air of the little boxes.

On the way home, the lucky ones with a ha'penny or a penny to spend usually stopped at the little baker's shop on the corner, and the woman filled their outstretched jerseys, which they held out like a miniature tarpaulin, with broken biscuits. You didn't get a paper bag for a ha'penny or a penny purchase, and anyway we all felt it was *far* better value to get handfuls tossed into a baggy jersey, and there was always plenty for all of us. The biscuits were mostly plain, but what a find to discover a cream fragment among the digestives!

Later, when we had swimming lessons at school, the

baths seemed quite different at three o'clock in the afternoon, and although we now had proper swimming instruction and learned to keep ourselves afloat, it lacked the magic of the morning visits.

Later still, as we grew older, we would go along in the evening, and again the atmosphere was entirely changed. Standing in the lamp-lit street, queuing to get in, we would hear the voices and shouts of those already in the pond, sounds which echoed strangely into the glass roof. And when we finally got inside, the bath looked so different under artificial lighting that we wondered uneasily if it could indeed be the scene of our childish ploys.

It was about this time that we penetrated the mystery of the other side of the bath building. We were getting too big now for the zinc bath at home, and were given fourpence on Fridays to have a hot bath. This was indeed luxury. The fourpence admitted us to the delicious warmth of the cubicles, and provided a rough towel for drying. There were degrees of grandeur, and a first-class bath cost ninepence. But beyond seeing a softer, whiter, fluffier towel, I never discovered what other delights were in store. Spending more than fourpence on a bath was forever beyond both purse and imagination.

There was always a queue, and we sat on wooden benches alongside the cubicles and enjoyed watching the leisurely movements of the woman attendant as she swished water along the stone floors to keep them clean, and we listened dreamily as she bade slow bathers to 'Hurry up, there's mair than you wantin' in the night'.

There were no taps on the baths, only projecting pieces of metal which had to be turned with the attendant's iron key. This was no doubt to prevent extravagance and overflowing, but the result of having no control over the water could be agonizing. No matter how accurately one felt the temperature of the water had been judged, when one had been asked to 'See if this is aw right', the moment the attendant disappeared, and one submerged the body gingerly, it was only too painfully brought home that judgement had been badly at fault, and there would be a yell as the scalding water reached the tenderness of the waist, and an imploring screech, 'Oh come *back*, missus, ah'm bein' roastit.' The attendant, used to such behaviour, ignored the cries as long as possible, partly to teach us a lesson and partly because she had duties elsewhere, but when she could stand the shouting no longer she would return, fling open the door with her pass-key and stand glaring balefully in the doorway. A towel would be hastily draped round the scarlet torso, as she fiercely turned on a jet of cold water. 'Noo, pit yer feet in this time, you silly wee besom, and make sure it's cauld enough,' she would command, adding: 'Fur ah'm no' comin' back *again*. Ah've the hale baths tae attend tae, an' ah'm no' dancin' attendance on you, so don't think it!'

Meekly a toe would be thrust from the folds of the

towel, and the water tested. 'Oh aye, it's a' right this time', and she would depart, muttering, 'It better be!'

If a mistake had been made a second time, it just had to be endured. To face that woman's wrath twice was not to be contemplated. So if the water was still too hot, the only solution was to press the cold spray above the bath into service. This was infuriatingly slow and never seemed to make the least difference to the temperature of the water, and the moment those waiting outside heard the spray, they knew what had happened and there would be shouts, 'Hurry up you, are you in there fur the night!'

The soap was coarse and yellow, the floor was stone, and the towel was hard, but what luxury it seemed to be able to wallow in a long 'wally' bath, and feel a gentle sleepiness steal over one as familiar voices rose and fell on every side, and chums called to each other through the partitions.

There were squeals of mock terror when the final cold spray was applied to keep one from catching cold on the way home, and beatific smiles on our pink steamy faces when we at last emerged, scrubbed, rinsed and dried, and more than ready for a penny-worth of chips to eat as we walked home.

Nine

We didn't manage to have a holiday every year, but when my mother decided that, yes, she thought she could maybe afford one this year, we talked of nothing else for weeks beforehand. We'd sit round the table when my mother came in from work at night and pore over the seaside advertisements in the paper. The ones which drew us like magnets were usually worded, 'Room and kitchen to let, Fair Fortnight, no linen supplied, attendance if desired, Low door, own key'. The lure lay in the last words. Low door, own key. A low door which opened on to a little side street that ran down to the sea. To us, born and reared in tenements, used to climbing miles of stairs in the course of the year, the excitement of walking right from the street over a threshold which led straight to the living-room was a thrill of which we never tired. It was almost like living on the exciting bustling pavement itself, and for my mother and Grannie it seemed like playing at house-keeping.

The minute we got out of the train we would race along the street ahead of Mother and Grannie, searching for the number of our own particular low door. Once, to my joy, our low door was fronted by a *red* doorstep. This was pure fantasy. I didn't know it was achieved by the use of red pipeclay, and I doubt if I would have believed it if anybody had told me. It was our magic seaside doorstep and I loved it. As soon as the door was opened, we children flew round the house, examining every drawer, every cupboard, the fancy taps on the sink, the fancy handles on the door. Everything was considered 'fancy' which differed from our own at home. While Mother and Grannie laid out our own clean linen and saw to the beds we were sent to the nearest shops to buy something for the tea.

Not for us the doubtful swank of sitting down to somebody else's cooking. We liked to buy and cook our own food. Why, the day might have been blighted from the start if we had been forced to accept what somebody else considered a suitable breakfast, which could be *kippers*, or, worse, *steamed fish*! It was always eggs for us, lovely fresh country eggs, for the country was no farther away than the end of the beach, and we could buy them from the farms any day. My mother had a whole egg, Grannie and I one between us, and the boys one between them, so half a dozen did us for two meals.

It was never any trouble to persuade us to run errands on holidays, for the shops were all so different from those at home. How absorbing it was to watch the man slice the bacon by hand instead of putting it into a machine. And didn't the milk taste more creamy and satisfying when it came out of a little tap on the side of a huge churn, carried on a cart, pulled by a donkey?

Chips from a cart lit by paraffin flares were twice as good as those from a shop, and what triumph to discover for ourselves a bakery which sold the crispest rolls in town, and which served them piping hot, in a bag with scarlet lettering, when we went down to buy them before breakfast each morning.

We worked cheerfully in the fields to help the farmer, regarding the whole thing as adventurous play, and were incredulous when we were given a bag of peas or strawberries as our reward. Our reward for what? For enjoying ourselves? This was paradise indeed. We were allowed by the farmer to go into the fields after the potato-pickers had finished, and keep for ourselves the tiny potatoes which had been left behind as too small to be worth lifting. With these my mother made chips for us, but we had to clean and scrape them ourselves, for she said they were far too fiddling for her. So the three of us would drape ourselves on top of sink and dresser, scraping and scrubbing the marble-sized potatoes, cutting them into minute slices, and at last, blissfully devour plates full of miniature fairy chips.

Seaside ice-cream had a taste all of its own too, served between wafers and biscuits intriguingly different from those at home. Some of the ice-cream may not even have been so good as our own Tallies in Glasgow, but it held fascination for us because it was different. Without ever being told, we knew it was the change which was the best part of our holiday.

The sea was a joy, of course, and distances so

impossible to measure in that wide expanse of ocean that I caused great amusement by vowing, the first day we arrived at Girvan, that I was going to paddle out to Ailsa Craig the minute I'd swallowed my tea. I refused to believe it was all of thirteen miles! And it only a wee speck on the map too, and practically joined to the coast.

How golden the sands were, after the earth of our tenement back courts. We made forts, and castles, and leaped from the wall running alongside, and turned somersaults of sheer delight, and after our games, discovered that salt water was far more buoyant than the baths at home, and we could swim satisfying distances without putting our feet down. When we came out, teeth chattering and blue with cold, my mother shuddered and wondered how we could find pleasure in such icy waters. But to have gone to the seaside and *not* gone into the sea would have been unthinkable, and we pitied the grown-ups who wouldn't take off their clothes and join us in our Spartan splashing.

The pierrots at the end of the sands provided glamorous entertainment. We never went inside the railed-off enclosure, of course, but pressed against the railings and drank in every word and noted every gesture. We loved each member devotedly, but never dreamt of asking for autographs. To us they were beings from another world, and it was unimaginable that we could speak to them. We went to every performance, and knew the repertoire as well as they did, but the moment one of the company came round with the little box for contributions, we vanished. We had no money to give away to people who seemed to us so rich and prosperous, and anyway the 'toffs' sitting inside the enclosure must have contributed *hundreds* of sixpences.

We would have stayed at the seaside all day long, but my mother and Grannie grew tired of sitting there, and we were taken into the countryside on long walks. It seemed all wrong to be walking away from the sea, but soon we were climbing trees, and searching for wild flowers, and hoping Grannie would soon decide she must have a glass of milk and a wee rest. This meant the treat of a visit to a farmhouse, with milk 'straight from the cow' and, on very special occasions, cakes and scones to go with the milk. These treats usually came almost at the end of the holiday, when my mother would look into her purse, count up her money, and decide it was safe to have a little spree. We had already paid for our wee house, so all that was left in the purse was spending money.

And always, on the last day of the holiday, we went to one of the big local houses which had a card on the gate saying, 'Flowers for sale – a shilling a bunch.' We were allowed to stroll round the garden, and Grannie and I made a slow and careful selection of beautiful, scented, old-fashioned cottage flowers to take back with us to our tenement, to remind us of the happy days spent in our own dear wee house, with its low door and its own key.

We always came home on a Saturday morning, to give us plenty of time to get in some food for the weekend, and to give my mother opportunity to get her dungarees ready for her work in the Railway wagon-shop on Monday morning.

Springburn, where I was born and brought up, depended for its existence on Railways and their equipment. We children were proud to think that our mothers and fathers had helped to build the wonderful engines we watched roaring away under the bridges to far-away London, to Sheffield and to Aberdeen. There were other places too, places which were only names to us as we chanted the splendid titles of the engines and took note of their numbers in our little notebooks.

Widows deemed it the greatest good fortune to get a job as a carriage cleaner, and they devoted to the cleaning of the trains the same personal attention and thoroughness they showed in keeping their own spotless homes clean. They would stand back, affection in their eyes as they surveyed the sparkling train windows and well-brushed upholstery, and in their day there were no complaints of dirty trains.

As for the men, they never stopped discussing the finer points of engineering. It was their hobby as well as their bread and butter. They talked, breathed, ate and slept railways. My mother used to say scathingly that there were more engines built over the counter of the local pub than were ever built in the sheds, for they talked of nothing else.

The Calais, Cowlairs, Hyde Park — magic names which spelled pay-packets to the fathers and even the mothers of all my chums. The 'horns', as we called the hooters, took the place of alarm clocks in our community. We wakened to the 'quarter to' horn, we stole an extra eight minutes, clinging fast to sleep before the 'seven minutes' horn had us tumbling out on to the cold linoleum; and by the time the eight o'clock horn had gone, we had plunged gaspingly into the cold water from the tap and were vigorously rubbing our frozen cheeks to life with a rough towel.

My mother had already left by the 'quarter to' horn, and was on her way to Cowlairs, where she painted railway wagons. Hard, heavy work for a slight little creature like her, but she was glad to get it, with three of us to feed and house, plus Grannie, of course.

We loved her tales of the railway shops, of the pranks they played on the 'gaffer', of how she and her chum Lizzie would hide underneath the wagons until he had gone past, so that they could indulge their passion for tea from the Thermos, and French cakes when they could afford them, consumed in the firm's time. There were no canteens in those days, and no 'breaks', and any nourishment was strictly unofficial. We shivered with fear as she told of near escapes, for we certainly thought discovery would have meant the sack — a dreaded word in the tenements.

She would describe in detail the vastness of the twelve-tonners and the sixteen-tonners, and the difference this made to the arm-stretching and reaching, and therefore to the speed of the work if they were given too many sixteen-tonners in proportion to the smaller wagons. I used to go along to the gate to meet her on pay nights, when the air was filled with chattering and laughing, as she and her workmates tumbled out, glad of the comfort of the pay-packet safely tucked into the top pocket of their dungarees. On the way home, reckless with a week's pay, we all went into Charlie's, the Italian shop on the corner, and tucked into the delights of sugar or nougat wafers. Nobody worried about spoiling the appetite for the meal awaiting them at home. It was the end of the week, they only had Saturday morning's work ahead of them, with maybe a dance on Saturday night and all day Sunday to relax. There was no hurry. They were all working. Life was good.

Sometimes my mother had to go on night-shift, and we grew used to seeing her come in at breakfast-time as we were getting ready for school. Her face and hands would be daubed with the paint she had been too tired to remove before she left the workshop, and her eyes closed with weariness as she sipped her tea.

Before taking this job in the paint-shop she had worked a machine at Hyde Park, where they made the big locomotives. She was very proud of her skill with the strong steel shapes, and sad when they had to sack all the women workers to make room for the men who needed the jobs. They made no fuss, the widows, at being ousted in this way. They accepted the fact that in normal conditions man was the bread-winner, and quietly looked elsewhere for work.

It was a tremendous excitement for us children when one of the big locomotives was ready for its journey through our streets to the docks, there to be shipped to China, or India, or some similar far-off land which knew, of course, that we made the best locomotives in the world. The huge iron gates of the works would swing open, and with the sure telepathy of children for knowing what was happening, we would be there clustered on the pavement, watching with bright-eyed interest and admiration as the gigantic locomotive was eased with deceptive skill on to its waiting trailer. It was a splendid thing of shining steel, beautiful in shape, and full of strength. The men who had fashioned her would spit casually to hide their pride in their workmanship, and the unemployed who joined us on the pavements would straighten their shoulders, for they believed and knew that they too were part of this great engineering tradition of Glasgow and of Scotland.

Because of its weight and size, it had to travel very slowly over the cobbles, vibrating the dishes on our shelves, and we whooped and cheered every inch of the way, only turning back when we were frighteningly far from our own familiar streets.

At lunch-time the horns were the signal for our streets to be filled with the crunch of hundreds upon hundreds of tramping feet as the railway workers hurried home for their dinner. No canteen meals for them.

They all worked within walking distance of a hot meal, and we ducked among them on our way home from school, avoiding many a half-hearted cuff on the ear as we nearly tripped them up. Wives had to have everything ready on time, and could tell to a second when their men would be turning in at the close, and mounting the stairs. Nobody used buses or trams, so there was no confusion over time-tables. Everybody walked, and dictated his own turn of speed.

After lunch, they didn't go in through the big gates until the final horn summoned them. It was their habit to squat down on their haunches along the walls flanking the works, smoking a final cigarette, studying their newspapers, or just enjoying a joke with each other, making the most of their last few minutes of leisure before the horn drew them to their feet and back to their machines.

They had skill in their hands, and the pride of the craftsman in their eyes, and my mother agreed with them when they declared that each steam loco had a personality of its own. Anyone who ever saw them taking the road out of our big works would know that. Each engine bearing its proud name, its boilers all ready to send sparks and smoke like a miniature volcano into the night, once its willing acolytes were in attendance. And we children felt a great sense of pride in these giants, for hadn't our mothers and fathers helped to create them?

The horns didn't sound on Sundays, and on that day

we had to learn to look at the clock again. My mother had a long lie on Sunday mornings, for it was the one day of the week she hadn't to be up early for work. Grannie put on her white apron and got out the big bowl, and baked the most mouth-watering scones and pancakes in case anybody dropped in for tea. And we children played in bed till the baking was finished, and then fought and scrambled to get into the zinc bath in front of the fire, and enjoy splashing in hot soapy water. We took it in turns to be bathed, and I was usually first, and my hair was washed too, and my brothers would lather it with soap until they could pull my front curls into a stiff point, like a rhinoceros horn, and I'd pretend to stab them as they drew a foot through the turbulent waters. Then I'd be whisked out, and more hot water was added for my brothers, from the kettles Grannie kept filled on top of the range. At the end of all this, the bath was rinsed and dried and put away for another week. In winter we dried our hair before the glowing fire in the range, but in summer we were sent down to the back court to let the sun adorn us with shining caps of curls. And afterwards, everything revolved round the church. What an enormous place this took in our lives.

As a four-year-old, I was trotted solemnly off to the morning service by the neighbours' older children, my penny or ha'penny clutched tightly in my hand. How important I felt as I dropped the coin into the plate when it came round, proud to be copying the actions of the big girls. I would gaze at the lofty ceiling, which I was sure reached right to heaven itself, and then turn my fascinated stare to the stained glass windows, almost drowning in their rich jewel-like colours. The minister's voice rose and fell, but I heard nothing of the message. The atmosphere of church was soothing and mysterious, and I loved every minute of it.

Later, I went to Sunday School with my brothers, and this was a much more light-hearted affair. Each class occupied a portion of a pew, with the teacher perched on the desk facing us, and thrilling us with stories from the Bible. We had little coloured texts to memorize for each week, and we studied the catechism and the creed. I was very worried about having to say 'I believe in the Holy Catholic Church'. How could I believe in this, when I was a Protestant and a Presbyterian at that? I felt this was betrayal of the most terrifying order, and could never get a truly satisfying explanation which my conscience would accept.

The flowing language of the Bible stirred me, and it was no trouble to memorize whole passages. Indeed at one time I actually committed to memory the entire book of Luke in preparation for a special examination. It was like learning a play, and the answers fell into place so aptly I walked off with the prize, to Grannie's delight. She was sure I was going to be a minister, and felt this was a splendid antidote to my passion for play-acting, which could come to no good.

Later still, I was old enough to join the Bible Class,

and at the same time I plunged into the activities of the Girl Guides, while my brothers were by this time in the Boys' Brigade. Getting the uniforms presented a bit of a problem, with our limited budget, but we made toffee apples and sold them to raise cash, and we found older boys and girls who were only too pleased to let us have their outgrown uniforms at bargain prices.

These uniforms were cleaned and polished to perfection for Church Parades, when the eyes of the entire congregation were on us as we formed into fours and then twos and marched down the centre aisle to fill almost the whole of the downstairs pews. There was no question of mothers or grannies helping us. It was all part of the discipline and the fun to wash and iron our ties, press the uniforms and polish belts and shoes, and Grannie watched this activity with a vigilant eye, amused at our industry, but full of encouragement of this excellent training in looking after ourselves. 'Aye, learn young, learn fair,' she would say, 'it's a grand thing to be independent.'

We weren't sure if Grannie and my mother would let us go with the Guides and the Boys' Brigade to summer camp. There would be billy-cans to buy, and mugs, and sand-shoes, and about a pound needed for the ten days' holiday, and the train fare. It seemed a fortune. 'Well, if you can each save up the pound you can go,' my mother at last announced. From that moment on we were in a whirl of excitement. We ran messages for neighbours, we gave special back-court concerts, we organized jumble-sales, and we made and sold trays and trays of tablet to those better off than ourselves. This delicious Scottish confection was a great favourite. Firmer than fudge, but not hard like toffee, it melted in the mouth. The piles of pennies grew and were changed to shillings, then into ten-shilling notes, and at last we had a whole pound each. The boys were going to Ayr and we were going to Berwick. We didn't need an alarm clock or a 'horn' to waken us on the morning of departure. We were up as soon as it was daylight. The sun was shining. We shivered with excitement. Grannie and my mother checked again and again that we had our pyjamas, a change of socks and underwear in our haversacks, and that our billy-cans and mugs were safely fastened to the outside strap. 'Noo mind and behave yersels,' they called after us as we clattered down the stairs, to meet with our companies outside the church. We were off. The officers had gone on ahead to see that the bell tents were erected, and we caught our breaths at the sight of those lofty tents spread over soft green grass, like a scene from Shakespeare's Agincourt we thought. We ate in one big marquee, and how good everything tasted eaten under canvas and in the company of our chums. It was a complete novelty to us to eat in company like this, outside our own homes, and our eyes met over the half-cold food, pleased with the strangeness of it all.

I was somewhat taken aback to find we had to take turns in the cook-house, and this meant not only cooking, but lighting the fire between an improvised fireplace of bricks. I trembled with fright at the responsibility of providing sustenance for all those hungry youngsters, *and* officers. I needn't have worried. Grannie's good teaching stood me in splendid stead, and once my cooking had been tasted, I was detailed to kitchen duties for the rest of the camping holiday. I didn't really mind. I was flattered that they should like my catering so much. Mass approval was more than I had ever expected, and I put it down to the fact that they couldn't all have grannies who were so expert as mine in giving us tasty and delicious food for next to nothing. And I had a few enviable privileges. All parcels sent down by more affluent mothers went straight to the kitchen. Oh the bliss of an unexpected pineapple tart sent down by a fond mamma and shared with me. This was a bonus to make the mouth water.

One of the surprising rules at this camp was that we must lie down on our sleeping mats and rest for an hour after lunch. This seemed to us quite hilarious. Big girls of twelve lying down during the day! We, who ran about from dawn till dusk at home, fitting in shopping, baby-minding, housework and a dozen other ploys between and after school, to need a rest on holiday! We couldn't lie still for laughing the first day, much to the officers' annoyance. But soon we grew quiet, and that lovely hour became something we looked forward to, and gave us a springboard for the rest of the day's activities.

When we came home from that first camp, a chum and I arranged a game of tennis for two o'clock the next day, for we were still in school holidays, and we couldn't understand why we were creeping about the courts yawning and half-dead. After a holiday too. There must be something wrong with us. And then it hit me with a blinding flash. This was the hour when we usually had our rest and already our bodies had formed the habit, and resented being asked to rush about. I was stunned at how quickly a habit, good or bad, can be formed.

As well as the Guides, we filled every seat at the Band of Hope and the Christian Endeavour meetings. The Band of Hope was splendid. We had lantern lectures, and learned the terrible dangers of picking up handkerchiefs in the street, which might be germ-infested. We absorbed gravely the examples of the evils of strong drink. We could see this every Saturday in the tenements, but it drove the lesson home, seeing it up there on the slides, and noting with a shudder every detail of the poor wives and children being thrown into the street because the husband had drunk away the rent money.

In lighter mood we were entertained by visiting artists playing the violin with what seemed to us superb expertise, and singers who sang 'The Floral Dance' and 'The Bold Gendarmes' so beautifully, we made the rafters ring with our applause.

I can't remember much about Christian Endeavour

meetings, except that we seemed to collect cash for every sick person in hospital, and I was sometimes thrillingly allowed to accompany the secretary with a basket of fruit or a box of sweets on the visit to the patient in hospital. I had to have a note to get off school for this journey, and I could never understand my teacher's barely suppressed smile when I said that we had raised the money through Christian Endeavour. It may have had something to do with the fact that I'd never seen the words written down and pronounced them 'Christian and ever'.

The church activities went on and on, catering for every age, and soon it was my turn to teach in Sunday School and perch on the pew and tell the little ones stories. They listened to me with wide eyes as I acted out the parables, and stammered and gulped with shyness when I made them tell me the stories in their own words. They were very poor, and I decided to save and give them a party in our house. They talked about this for weeks, and when I took them home after Sunday School on the day we'd arranged, their torn jerseys were washed and pressed, their hair slicked down with water, and their shabby boots shining with boot polish. It was the simplest fare, for I only had two shillings a week pocket money out of which I'd saved for this feast, but the table looked festive with my mother's china set out on a snowy cloth. These children only knew scrubbed tables or American cloth which could be wiped with a damp cloth, and were overawed at the sight of a real white tablecloth. We had salmon sandwiches, one tin eked out with lots of milk and margarine, but salmon was their favourite and a great luxury, and the mere smell of it set their mouths watering. We had jellies, and I'd baked apple tarts and a fruit cake. To finish up, we had a big dish of cheap sweeties and home-made tablet. When they'd finished the last conversation lozenge, one of the wee boys said it was just like the parable of the Prodigal Son – he'd never seen a fatted calf, but he was sure it was no better than my party.

My mother had been horrified at the idea of ten little boys stampeding into the house, but when she saw their eager eyes, and their appreciation of our humble catering, her eyes filled with tears, 'God love them,' she said, 'they're that easily pleased. Aye, of course you can taken them ben the room and play the gramophone for them.' This was the accolade, for only grown-ups were entertained in our 'room', which was kept like a shrine for special occasions, and I was as proud as if I'd been awarded the Victoria Cross. The 'room' made it a real Christmas party.

Ten

Time is very hard to measure when you are very young, and when we were children it was the windows of the big Cooperative up the road which told us that Christmas was near. Nobody at home mentioned it, for when you're working on a tight budget you don't go around encouraging your family to wild dreams of turkeys or extravagant toys and presents. You keep as quiet as possible, and try to forget the slimness of your purse, for however many letters are sent up the chimney to 'Santa', few are likely to find their way to your room and kitchen.

But the shops flashed the message from every window, and the news would quickly spread the moment the first spy noted that the blinds had been drawn on certain windows, to hide the activity going on behind. 'The Co's getting ready fur their Christmas windaes,' we chorused to each other. 'It must be gettin' near time to send a letter to Santa.' We wouldn't write a line, of course, until we'd seen what was newest in the way of toys and books. We were in a fever of impatience, and raced up the hill every half-hour to see if we could be first to see the blinds go up.

I was never first to see the exciting display as the

curtain rose, but I was certainly among the first in our tenement. One look at an excited face coming charging down the hill was enough. The blinds were up. I knew it. In a moment I was racing up Springburn Road on winged feet, like a Pied Piper, gathering children from every close as I ran. When we rounded the bend, and light from those magnificent windows spilled out on to the pavements, we automatically slowed down, the better to take in the general scene. It was a wild confusion to our eyes – colour, light, extravagant array of unbelievable toys – mountains of beautiful books – we drew a deep breath, and settled down to the bliss of examining each window item by item. Rapturous cries as we found the things we would love to have, if we were rich. 'Oh, isn't that doll *beautiful*!' I crouched low to the pavement, to make sure the enchanting creature had underclothes that I could take off and put on if she were mine. She had, and they were lace-trimmed! And little socks. And shoes with buckles. Oh, and the bonnet came off too. I felt life could hold nothing better than the prospect of holding that perfect replica of a baby in my arms. But of course I knew it was impossible. Still, I could run up and admire her every single day until somebody bought her. It was always such a long time to Christmas and there would be plenty of time for this satisfying window courtship.

Each of us chose an impossible dream like the baby doll before we got down to the realistic level of things our mothers just might be able to afford. We pretended it was Santa, but we knew better than to wish for things of an extravagant nature. There were plenty of other delights, though, and in exuberant mood we'd choose about half a dozen each, and we always included a brand-new Children's Annual. I don't know who bought the new ones which were in the shop windows, but we always seemed to get one which had been passed down by somebody else, its covers printed by a variety of grubby fingers, and with rubbed-out scribbles down the sides of the pages. We shook our heads virtuously over this defacing of the Annual. If *we* had ever had the good fortune to have had a new book, we'd *never* have put a mark on it. *Never.* More, we'd have put brown paper covers on it to protect the lovely shiny outside binding.

So we chose our beautiful new Annual through the window, and added other coveted treasures, but always with a watchful eye on the price ticket so that we could throw out suitable hints for our mother's consideration. The sighing over the Meccano sets, the huge Teddy-bears, the life-like dolls, the boxing gloves, the football boots, the train-sets, the scooters, and the skates, whispered away. We concentrated now, with the realism of the tenement child, on modest desires. 'Oh yes, that wee box of paints at one-and-six, that would be great, and it would go into my stocking too.' My eyes moved along, 'Oh and maybe that wee sewing set – I could embroider a flooer on Grannie's apron.' How much was it? I nearly turned a somersault to see the upside-down ticket. 'Two shillings!' No, it was too much. What else was there for a shilling, or one and sixpence. 'Oh gosh, I nearly didn't see it! A pencil-box with a little painted flower on the lid, for one-and-nine.' It was empty of course, but I had plenty of wee bits of pencil and rubber to fill it, and a treasured bone pen with a Waverley nib given to me by a neighbour when I'd run her messages for a whole week.

Our final choices made, the letters to Santa started. Grannie was sure we'd set ourselves on fire as we leaned dangerously over the range and tried to float our little notes right up the chimney. It was terribly bad luck if it weren't wafted up first time, or fell downwards into the flames. Grannie scorned such superstitious ways. 'Do you think Santy Claus kens whether yer letter fell doon or no'?' she'd demand. 'Awa' tae yer beds, afore ye burn yourself.' And, as we protested and wanted to write just one more note, she'd threaten, 'Another word oot o' ye, and I'll write a note to Santy Claus masel' an' tell him no' to bother comin' near this hoose, for I'll no' clean the flues to be ready for him.' This was enough. We crept to bed. Och we could always write a wee letter tomorrow night. There was plenty of time.

And then suddenly it was Christmas Eve and time to hang up our stockings. We had been on the go all day. I'd been sent down to the butcher to collect Grannie's favourite piece of sirloin. We never had a turkey, or a goose, or any of the larger birds. They were as far beyond our reach as caviare or nightingale's tongues, and we were entirely satisfied with our sirloin. We never had mince pies either. The first time I tasted one, it was a bitter disappointment. I thought mince meant meat, and I couldn't believe it when my teeth met a fruity mixture when I'd expected mince and gravy. How could anybody write so glowingly about Christmas mince pies, I thought in disgust, they weren't even as good as Grannie's ordinary fruit tarts.

My mother was late coming home on Christmas Eve. She did the toy-shopping straight from work, and there would be an exciting rustling as she thrust her purchases into the press in the lobby before coming into the kitchen for her tea. We asked no questions, but nearly burst with delight as our eyes met each other's.

It was an eternity before morning came. The stockings were hung along the mantelpiece, my long-legged hand-knitted stocking made by Grannie, held down by the big darkie bank, that smiling Negro head and shoulders, with the movable arm, and a hand which popped the pennies into his mouth. My brothers' stockings held down by the tea-caddy and the heavy alarm clock. I thought I hadn't been to sleep at all, but a movement in the kitchen as Grannie filled the kettle, sent my eyes flying open. It was still dark. 'Och light the gas, Grannie,' I pleaded. 'I'm waken.' 'It's only six o'clock,' she whispered back. 'I'm juist makin' a wee cup o' tea.' But she lit the gas, and handed my stocking into the bed. The boys heard us and came running through from their bed in the room. They climbed into the hurley bed beside me, and we all dived into the stockings. A wee toty doll for me, that I could make clothes for. Lovely! A wee sewing set for making the clothes – my eyes sparkled over the coloured threads. What was this now? Mmmm. A lovely big bar of chocolate, the sort I liked best. And pushed right into the toe of my stocking, a tangerine wrapped in silver paper. 'Noo, don't eat that chocolate afore yer breakfast,' Grannie warned, 'or you'll be sick.' As if I would! That was my treasure, to be broken off and eaten, piece by piece, during the day for as long as I could make it last. And I'd keep the tangerine for after my sirloin. The boys put their new cowboy belts on over their pyjamas, and fired their toy guns at Grannie and at me, and we all turned somersaults on the bed.

While we played, Grannie baked some scones and pancakes just as if it was Sunday, and we had them hot with our tea. Oh, Christmas morning was lovely. My mother wakened, and started to get ready for work, for there was no holiday on Christmas Day for her. Pointing to the mantelpiece, she said to me, 'Have you looked up there yet?' I gasped. There, quite unnoticed from the bed, was a luxury I'd never dreamed of owning. I'd put it on my wee letter to Santa, but only as a fantasy. A little toy piano. And my mother had somehow found the money for it. And beside it a set of toy soldiers for each of the boys. Now we knew the reason for all that overtime she'd worked. We could hardly speak for excitement. Carefully Grannie reached up and lifted the treasures down, and I tried to play 'God save the King' from the dozen notes of my piano. The boys ranged their soldiers in battle formation. Grannie sipped her tea and watched us, a twinkle in her eye. Oh, Christmas morning was more than lovely. It was perfect. We never had a tree, but we never missed it.

Everything was extra special to us at this splendid time of the year. After our simple diet, everything provided over and above ordinary meals spelt luxury. The Sunday School party, with its bag of tea-bread, and maybe a prize here and there for musical chairs or races, was a treat we looked forward to for weeks. I remember one terrible time Grannie had bought us new tin mugs, and we had them tied round our necks with tapes and I was warned to see that we didn't lose them. When the hot tea was poured into them the handles became scalding hot, and we couldn't hold them. There they were, tied to our necks full of boiling tea, with us leaping back kicking wildly to keep our legs from being scalded, while the tea cascaded to the floor. Oh, how ashamed we were, and it never occurred to us to take the tinnies off. So we lost our tea, and nobody thought to bring us a re-fill. And we didn't dare to ask. 'Aye,' said Grannie, when she'd reassured herself we weren't burned, 'that's the way to learn – by your mistakes. You'll no' be so daft anither time.' But she gave us a cup of tea when we came home.

And one year I had to learn, the hard way, not to ask for things before I ought to have them. The Cooperative window held a John Bull printing outfit which I coveted above all else. I was terrified somebody would buy it before Christmas. 'Och, get it now, Mother,' I urged. 'I don't want anything else, if you'll just get it now.' My mother held out as long as she could, and then grew tired of my nagging persistence. 'If I buy it now,' she warned, 'you'll get nothing else at Christmas, for I haven't the money for two presents.' It had been a lean year and I knew she spoke the truth. Oh, I didn't want anything else, I assured her, only the John Bull outfit. So she got it for me. And when Christmas came I'd used up the inked pad and all the special paper that came with it. And I didn't get anything else. That year the mantelpiece was bare of anything for me on Christmas morning.

Over the year we saved our precious pocket money to buy little things to give to Grannie and my mother. Acid drops for Grannie, or a wee bottle of Eau-de-Cologne. A quarter pound of chocolates for my mother or a hankie. One year I sent away to a magazine for a linen square about six inches by six inches, complete with transfer and coloured silks. The transfer was of a little crinolined figure, with poke bonnet and curls, and I thought it exquisite. I sewed it up in the hothouses of the public park, so nobody would know what I was doing. The materials cost two shillings – a fortune – and it took me months to finish it with its tiny stitching, for I had to do it so secretly and in my spare time after school. My mother was enchanted with this gift, especially when the park-keeper told her afterwards how it had been managed.

One useless gift, which I loved buying, but which cost me a whole year's savings, was a pale blue silk handkerchief sachet for my mother. I had to climb up on to the chair in the shop, so that I could gaze on the selection spread out for my inspection on the glass counter. I was dazed with the splendour laid before me, and refused to be persuaded to buy something more practical. I had run messages for a neighbour for a year to acquire this nest-egg, and I was determined that my mother should have something frivolous and beautiful. She didn't spoil it by telling me I had wasted my money, but somehow when I saw it in our tenement setting I knew I had, and I never saw her use it. It was kept in a drawer. The hankies my mother stowed in her dungarees' pocket were ill-suited to a pale blue silk sachet, and I know it now.

But if we didn't decorate the house for Christmas, we had a positive orgy of cleaning for Hogmanay. Grannie and I shone the steels on the range, the brass covers on the dresser, and the brass gas-bracket, door-knob and letter-box till they sparkled like gold. The flues were cleaned. The floor polished. My mother washed all the furniture in the room with vinegar water, polished the tiles on the fireplace till they looked like amber, and rubbed the polished mantelpiece – solid mahogany she assured us – to a gleaming satin. The 'room' was the best room in the house, and was in fact the only room apart from the kitchen where we ate, and lived, and where Grannie and I slept, and we were well disciplined to accept that in the 'room' we must not romp or play. We thought it beautiful, and it had for us the special air of a museum-piece. We shared our mother's anxiety that it should be kept nice for 'folk coming' and for special occasions, and the most splendid of all special occasions was Hogmanay. This was the only time food was brought into the room. At other times, nobody would have dared risk dropping food or drink on our best things. But at Hogmanay – ah! that was different. A table was set near the window, spread with our best white cloth, lace-trimmed, and on it was laid the best china. Plates were laden with Genoa cake (my mother's favourite), cherry cake, Dundee cake, a round cake of shortbread and shortbread fingers. There was a wee bit of black bun for those who liked it, but it was only the very oldest members of the company who seemed to enjoy nibbling it. We children never touched it. There was a tray with bottles of port, sherry and ginger wines. However poor the tenement people were, they could always manage a few bottles for Hogmanay. Glasses sat on another tray. On the sideboard the best crystal bowl was filled with oranges and tangerines for the Hogmanay visitors, and we gazed at them enviously, but would never have dreamt of touching them. I remember one Hogmanay a stray cat wandered into our best room just after my mother had arranged everything to her satisfaction, and when she went through later to have another peep to make sure she'd forgotten nothing, there was the brute sitting on the white tablecloth, clawing at the black bun! Her screech of horror brought us all running, and the cat disappeared in a streak of terror as we all leaped to rescue the rest of the food. Nobody got black bun that year.

When it grew dark my mother put a match to the fire in the grate, and soon the blaze was reflecting itself in the amber tiles, and everything was poised, in lovely cleanliness, waiting for the magic hour of midnight when the New Year would be ushered in.

We children were in our pyjamas by this time, and the minute the bells were announcing midnight, we were given a wee sip of home-made ginger wine and a bit of shortbread, then whisked off to bed in the kitchen. We would lie listening for the first-foots arriving, and we'd fall asleep to the sound of conversation and doors opening and shutting, and shouts of 'Happy New Year, an' mony o' them'. Occasionally a voice could be heard in the lobby, asking, 'Are the weans in their bed? Och here's something for their pocket. Gi'e it to them in the morning,' and sleepily we would wonder if it would be a threepenny bit or a sixpence that we'd have for our darkie bank when we wakened up.

On New Year morning I always took Grannie down to see her 'chum' a short tram ride away. But before we went, we made sure the room was tidied up, and the tables re-set with the food and the wines for the folk who would drop in during the day to wish us a Happy New Year. My mother would be at home to welcome them, for she didn't have to go to work on New Year's Day, which was always a holiday.

I helped Grannie to put on her good black shoes, and I fastened the pin of the black cameo she wore at the neck of her best black silk blouse, and saw that the blouse was tucked in right the way round inside the waist of her long dark grey skirt. Then on top went her dark coat, and last of all her hat with its winter trimming of cherries was set carefully on her silvery hair, at an angle which wouldn't disturb the wee bun at the back. She looked entirely different from our workaday grannie, and I was transformed from my schoolday self in my navy blue reefer coat, long black stockings and, best of all *shoes*, not boots. The shoes, I felt, gave me a most ladylike appearance. My black velour hat was held on with a good piece of elastic, which kept it firmly anchored at windy corners, and my curls were brushed neatly over my shoulders. When we reached the tram, where it stood waiting at the terminus, there always seemed to be a drunk man sitting inside, half-asleep, softly singing 'The Star o' Rabbie Burns', and for ever afterwards I always associated the name of Burns with New Year revelries. When she heard the man singing, Grannie would smile and sing herself, 'We'll a' be prood o' Robin'. The man's heavy lids would lift to Grannie, delighted by her approval, and he would be encouraged to break into a spirited rendering of 'Robin was a rovin' lad'. The variation in names, Rabbie, Robin, puzzled me, but Grannie assured me that both applied to our poet Burns, and she herself was gey fond of the name Robin for him, as she felt it suited him better.

We told the conductor where to let us off, and he stopped the tram long enough to let us get down without splashing our stockings or Grannie's skirt, and then we crossed the road to the tenement where Grannie's chum lived. We reached a beautifully polished door on the landing and rang the bell. A soft shuffle told us she was coming, and then I was being embraced in a flurry of soft arms and incredibly soft face and we were bustled into the kitchen. At this time Grannie was about sixty and her friend about seventy-five, so she seemed truly ancient to me. She wore a snowy white cap with a fluted frill, and her black dress was protected by a large white apron. When she spoke, her voice was so soft I had to lean right forward to hear what she said. She might have stepped straight out of the pages of *Little Red Riding Hood* and I was fascinated. She in her turn was filled with wonder over me, and how lively I was, and how quick, and she kept turning and looking at me again and again as she got out plates and glasses and wine.

The kitchen was full of knick-knacks and shining brass, and there were little lace covers on all her chairs. Occasionally, to Grannie's horror, I seized the poker as a prop when I sang them a song from a pantomime, but their favourite was 'Bonnie Mary of Argyle' which always brought a tear to their eyes, I never knew why.

There was an old-fashioned horn gramophone which wheezed out the songs of Harry Lauder, and I'd reduce the two old ladies to scandalized laughter when I imitated him afterwards. It must have been a long time since the old lady had entertained children, for she seemed to have no idea of what was suitable. I was handed a glass of port to sip when she poured out one for Grannie and herself. Grannie either didn't notice or was too polite to interfere, and I was forced to take tiny sips of this horrid-tasting liquid and pretend it was as nice as my mother's delicious ginger wine. Later, the strong tea nearly took the skin off my tongue, and Grannie frowned at me when I screwed up my nose. But the sandwiches and cakes were delicious, although the two old ladies didn't seem to have much interest in them. I was amazed that they seemed to get more pleasure from that terrible wine and the strong tea.

Afterwards, I brought Grannie home, taking great care to see that she got on and off the tramcars safely. She only went out twice a year, at the Fair and at Hogmanay, so she wasn't used to traffic. I nearly burst with pride at being her escort, and we had to stop every few yards for the neighbours to admire her outfit and to wish her 'Happy New Year'. When we got home her lovely shoes were put away in their cardboard box. Her coat was hung up and left to air before being stowed at the back of the wardrobe, where it would stay until it was brought out for her to wear at the Fair. Her skirt was folded over a hanger, the black silk blouse put away with tissue paper, and there was my dear familiar grannie again, picking up her knitting needles and getting on with a sock while she told my mother all about our outing. When my mother asked if I'd behaved myself, I held my breath and wondered if Grannie would mention how free I had been with the poker, but she just glanced at me, and assured my mother, 'Oh aye, she did fine. She's quite gettin' to be the lady.' I gazed at her gratefully, but wondered if Grannie *really* believed I was getting to be a lady. I had heard her say often enough that folk were inclined to live up to the descriptions they heard of themselves, and maybe she hoped I'd try to be a lady, and leave other folks' pokers alone in future. Yes, that must be it.

The magic of the New Year lasted quite a long time, with even the postman being invited in for a glass of something and a piece of cake. But we knew it was over when one day we went into the room and the tablecloth and the food had vanished. It was back to school for us then, and back to the workaday world for the tenement, but our pleasure in the Hogmanay revels kept us warm for many a long winter day afterwards. In the tenements we accepted cheerfully that it had to be auld claes and parritch after the feasting.

Eleven

I remember vividly my first deliberately social visit to 'the town', as we called the centre of Glasgow. Not for messages. Not with the gird. But just to be part of the grown-up world. Until that day, the boundaries of my world stretched from Bishopbriggs to Castle Street, with sometimes a dizzy venture to Campsie on holiday Mondays, when the route was filled with wonder. The long stretches of untenanted country, the wee row of miners' cottages, so different from our high tenements, the canal flowing placidly below fearfully averted eyes. We had been well warned to fear this canal. Terrible tales were told of disobedient children who had fallen in, never to be seen again. These stories of the dangers of water made such a strong impression on me that once, when crossing the 'steps of Kelvin', which were just large boulders to let us cross the river at that point, I took off my long-legged boots and slung them round my neck, so that if I did fall into the water, the weight of the boots wouldn't drag me down. As I stood on one of the boulders, it wobbled, and I shrieked and fell to my knees. To my horror, one of my new boots fell into the river, and floated away. I was about to leap after it, when a man on the bank shouted, 'Let it go, better a boot than a child.' These dramatic words shocked me back to my original terror of the water, and he had to wade out and guide me over to the bank. I raced down the path, and could see my boot, so near and yet so far, and I wept as I wondered what my mother would say. I was so distraught that instead of leaving both boots off, and going about in my bare feet till I could get home, I put on the one boot I had saved, and hopped about now on a bare foot, now on a boot, until my legs ached from the uneven progress. Later that night when I told my mother what had happened, she sighed, and weakly agreed it was better to have let the lost boot perish. She knew that a twenty-five and sixpenny pair of boots bought the previous day now had to be replaced from her two pounds ten a week pay, and maybe in her heart of hearts felt that in the interests of economy I might have attempted a brave little rescue of the boot, without too much danger to life and limb. I sensed her divided feelings when, on repeating the man's words, 'Better a boot than a child', for the third time, she cuffed me on the ear and said irritably, 'Oh, don't be so dramatic. Go to bed.' My poor mother. Half a week's wages lost because of my carelessness.

At the other end of my boundary was Castle Street, with its unknown back courts, and evil-smelling chimney dominating the chemical works. In between, lay romantic sounding Fountainwell Road, where I wept at an old lady's sink when I heard the story of how her only son had been killed on the very day of the Armistice of the First World War. This seemed to me a fate too cruel to be borne, and I wondered how she ever laughed again. Although I was a staunch Rechabite, I couldn't find it in my heart to condemn the old lady for seeking comfort in the 'bottle' when she thought of her poor son. My mother found out about those visits and stopped them at once. I was sorry, for I found the proximity of Fountainwell Road to the graveyard very mysterious, and somehow a fitting background to the sad story of the soldier son.

Nearby was another strange piece of territory known as the Hunts. The full name was Huntingdon Square, and this was a large square courtyard quite different from our oblong affairs, and providing limitless expanses of concrete for ball-beds, skipping ropes, peever, and all the childish games dear to my heart. And although we were timid about invading other back courts, the concrete courtyard of the Hunts was an irresistible temptation with its perfect surface for these games. Never was peever manipulated so skilfully, never ball stotted so high, as in the courtyard of the Hunts. It was worth the risk of being chased by the big boys and girls who rightfully played there, to know the fulfilment of such expert playing.

These then were my boundaries until the day of the students' collection for charity, when I suddenly stunned my two chums by suggesting we went into the town to see the start of the parade. I don't know where the idea came from. Perhaps the chrysalis was ready to burst its case, and the time was ripe for me to venture forth into a wider world. Until I actually said the words, I'd had no idea that I must subconsciously have been moving towards this moment. But, once uttered, we were all three passionately determined that the idea must be carried out.

We would walk, of course. The thought of spending money on fares was too ludicrous to be entertained. We would each save ninepence. That would allow three-pence for a cup of coffee, and fourpence for two cakes. I knew these prices from my mother, who occasionally gave herself this treat with a fellow-worker. The remaining tuppence we'd give to the students for their charity.

At this time my pocket money for spending was threepence a week, and even with the odd ha'penny or penny earned from affluent adults for running down for a packet of cigarettes or a forgotten ounce of tobacco, it would take a few weeks to manage a clear ninepence. But I was in no hurry. This adventure to town was something to savour, and the brilliance of the idea of dining out was still so staggering I needed a bit of time to see myself actually doing it. I wanted to rehearse every move in my own mind.

I had never been inside a tearoom. My only experience of such things was on the screens of the cinema, where the heroine walked boldly in, accompanied by the man of her choice, sat down and ate large and wonderful meals. I shivered with apprehension and delight every time I thought of walking in and ordering coffee and cakes, but how actually to do it was beyond imagination.

When one of my chums told her mother of our plan, that good lady was horrified at my presumption. She was sure such grandiose ideas in one so young boded ill for my future. 'Who are you,' she demanded, 'to suppose grown women are there to attend to your wants?' But if they were waitresses, I thought, surely they must want customers. But, of course, I was much too confused to argue with her.

Still, she put a terrible doubt in my heart, and all the way on that walk to town I felt a sinking in my stomach when I thought a derisive waitress might refuse to serve me because I was too soon aspiring for attention. I need have had no such fears. I led the way and we sat down at a table. 'Three cups of coffee,' I ordered huskily, 'and six French cakes.'

The waitress took us in at a glance. 'Imphm,' she said, 'I suppose you know they're tuppence each?' This was language we understood. 'Aye,' I assured her, 'we've each got sevenpence.' We'd never heard of tipping, and anyway would have considered it madness to give money to somebody wh) was clearly much better off than we were, and gettin ₁ good wage every week.

We had never tasted coffee before, and weren't sure if we would like it, but we could get tea at home and we felt this was far too ordinary to choose in this magnificent glass-bedecked salon. We peeled the paper carefully off our French cakes, determined not to lose a morsel of the icing, which was apt to stick treacherously if treated too roughly.

When we had savoured the last crumb we leaned back, ecstatic and replete, and watched the students cavorting in the street below. Some gaudily clad males actually came into the tearoom and raced upstairs in search of us, lured by our eager faces pressed to the windows. They were obviously disappointed to find gym slips and black lisle stockings. We each dropped our tuppence into the outstretched boxes with an air of abandon. It was a tremendous gesture to give tuppence away like this, for we longed for another French cake, and then we called for the bill. I collected the seven-pences from my chums and paid over the staggering sum of one and ninepence for our feast. We knew it would cost exactly this sum, but somehow when the moment came for handing it over, we felt we had spent a fortune.

Next moment we were in the street, ready for the walk home. We gazed at each other in triumph. We had done it. We had come to town. We had eaten and drunk at a famous restaurant, and we had each donated tuppence to charity. We had lived. We turned our footsteps towards home, and drew deep breaths of utter satisfaction. It had been a marvellous adventure.

That winter was the last I was to know as a child. Grannie took her usual dose of bronchitis at the end of November, but this time she seemed strangely listless. During previous attacks she ruled the house from her bed, and I had to follow her instructions to the letter. The soups were made, the vegetables prepared, the table laid, all under her vigilant eye, and she ate and drank her little meals with a critical palate. We talked and argued, and I was praised or scolded, and we didn't worry too much about bronchitis, for the only difference was that instead of sitting in the big chair with her knitting, Grannie was in bed. And I was doing the cooking.

Now she was very still, and my mother, who had stayed off work, kept glancing at her with a troubled frown. For some reason, it seemed we had to speak in whispers. 'Does Grannie want any dinner?' I asked, when my mother had poured the soup. 'You see if she wants any,' my mother said. I went over to the bed, and Grannie regarded me with frighteningly thoughtful eyes. When I asked if she wanted any soup she shook her head.

When I went over to the bed again, to see if maybe she would like a cup of tea and a biscuit, her eyes looked withdrawn, but she thought she could fancy a nice cup of tea. 'Nane o' yer sleesh,' she whispered. 'A guid strong cup noo'. That sounded more like my grannie, and I quickly got it ready. But she was too weak to lift the cup to her lips and I, who was never allowed to help Grannie in this way, for she scorned softness, had to put my hand behind her shoulders, and take the cup to her mouth. This was surely a terrible dose of bronchitis, and I wished the doctor would come again.

He came in after lunch, and he sounded her chest

and took her hand. 'Now, now, Grannie, what's this you've been up to? You'll have to take your soup, you know. You must have something to stick to your ribs.' She managed a smile for him, and I was shooed away from the bed. Surely he wouldn't talk to Grannie like that if she were really ill? She was just tired. That was it. How often had I heard her say, as she moved about our kitchen, doing a hundred and one different jobs, 'Aye, the willin' horse gets the heaviest burden to bear.' And she would laugh when I would say, 'Whit horse dae ye mean, Grannie? Is it Sanny the horse that helps at the smiddie?'

My mother decided to sit up all night, which made me tremble, for I knew people only did this when illnesses were serious. I was put into the big bed, in case I'd disturb Grannie in the hurley. I didn't go to the penny matinée that Saturday, for Grannie would only take her gruel or her tea if I gave it to her. It was a dream. Me ministering to Grannie instead of her doing it to me.

In the morning, Sunday morning, when I wakened and looked down at the hurley to see if she was any better, Grannie was lying, pale and remote, with her eyes shut and I knew that she was dead.

I was prostrate with grief that I was too young to express, and it was decided it would be easier for everyone if I were out of the way until after the funeral. It had to be somewhere not too far from school, for there was no spare cash for expensive tram or bus fares, and as we were in the grip of winter I couldn't walk far.

And so, as Auntie Jeanie's house fulfilled these requirements, we accepted her offer to put me up. I could sleep with Betty and would be no trouble, she assured my mother.

I had never slept at anybody's house before, apart from holiday apartments, so I was quite unaware of the upset even one extra person can give to a household. In my numb misery I didn't even begin to appreciate Auntie Jeanie's generosity in offering to have me in addition to her own three children, and I went listlessly to the new address after school finished at four o'clock. I don't remember that first evening at all. I suppose I must have done some homework, have eaten something and finally gone to bed, but nothing of that remains in my memory. But the morning! Ah! that was different!

With Grannie I'd been accustomed to being roused almost as soon as she got up herself, and while the fire was being lit I was getting dressed, and swiftly off to the shops for the rolls for breakfast, and maybe some mince for our midday meal, which we called our dinner, and possibly whisking along to the fruit-shop for some vegetables for soup.

I'd pull my hand-knitted jersey over my head, lace up my long-legged boots, and at the same time reel off a list of the things I thought Grannie might want. I'd get the purse out of the kitchen drawer, seize the basket and be off, almost before Grannie had time to agree that I'd remembered everything. Sometimes, in winter, when I had chilblains, it took me an age to drag my aching heels to the shops and back, and I would stop at every iced puddle and splinter the mica-thin brittle surface with my boot. The fun of this nearly made me forget the agony of the chilblains, but then the pain would come flaming back and it would seem certain that I must be late for breakfast and for school.

Once the house was safely reached, I'd sit on the long stool and toast the rolls in front of the fire, which by now was blazing in the open range. One for Tommy, one for Willie, and a half each for Grannie and for me, which was all we wanted. As each was toasted, I would run to the scrubbed sink top with it, cut open the steaming centre, plop in a slice of margarine, and watch with pleasure as the yellow melting fat ran into the hot dough. A smart tap on the crisp top as I shut the roll cracked the surface satisfactorily in all directions, and it was popped on a plate on top of the range to keep warm while I toasted the others.

Grannie meanwhile had been making the porridge, and infusing the tea, and soon we three children were kneeling on the rug with our porridge bowls on top of the long stool which ran the length of the fireplace, the heat from the fire warming our faces and fingers as we supped the good meal. How cosy these winter breakfasts were, for we had all been out of doors to whet our appetites, the boys delivering their milk round, and of course me getting the messages in.

I had thought this routine would go on for ever, for I knew no other.

But now Grannie was dead, and here was I in a strange bed in a strange kitchen. I lay silent and still in my misery, waiting for a voice to tell me it was time to get up and go for the rolls. I wondered where Auntie Jeanie bought hers, and if I would be able to find the shop quickly, and get back in time to make my way to school before nine o'clock, for I would have farther to walk from this house.

I opened my eyes, and to my amazement Auntie Jeanie was standing by the bed with a tray. A tray! And on it was a cup of tea, a bowl of porridge and a buttered roll. I stared uncomprehendingly. 'Who's no' weel?' I asked. 'Is it Betty?' And I turned to the sleeping figure beside me to search for signs of flu or fever.

'No, no,' said Auntie Jeanie comfortably, 'it's for you, pet. It's your breakfast.' 'But there's naethin' wrang wi' me,' I said in bewilderment. 'And whit aboot the messages?' It was Auntie's turn to look surprised. 'What messages?' she asked.

When I explained that I always went for the shopping before breakfast, to make sure Grannie would have everything before I went to school, she looked round at her three children who were now awake and listening with interest to our conversation. 'Do you hear that?' she demanded. 'You three don't know you're born, that's clear.' Then, turning to me, she smiled, 'Well, no messages this morning, my lass. Eat your breakfast in bed, like the other three, and see if we can get some colour into those pale cheeks.'

I was dumbfounded. They had breakfast in bed *every morning*! So I was to have breakfast in bed too. And no messages. The fire was lit, the kitchen a picture of cosy comfort. I should have envied my cousins their life of ease, and yet I felt only contempt for them. I could hear Grannie's voice as though she were in the room, 'Bairns have to learn to stand up to life and work hard, for we never ken whit's in front o' them.' I knew what her verdict would be on my cousins, 'Spoiled, that lot — fair spoiled.'

I trembled. Maybe I was being spoiled too, now that Grannie wasn't there to keep me strong for the battle. Maybe I wouldn't be able to face up to life if I went soft this way.

But for one morning, in the strangeness of Auntie Jeanie's house, and under the numbing weight of my sense of loss, I allowed myself to savour, for the very first time, the experience of having breakfast in bed. I condemned myself for my weakness and I hoped it would do my character no harm.

I whispered to the shadows, 'Just for this one morning, Grannie. I'll get up for it tomorrow.' And I did.

JEFF PEARCE

A POCKETFUL OF HOLES AND DREAMS

The poor boy who made his fortune . . . not just once but twice.

Little Jeff Pearce grew up in a post-war Liverpool slum. His father lived the life of an affluent gentleman whilst his mother was forced to steal bread to feed her starving children. Life was tough and from the moment Jeff could walk he learned to go door to door, begging rags from the rich, which he sold down the markets. Leaving school at the age of fourteen, he embarked on an extraordinary journey, and found himself, before the age of thirty, a millionaire.

Then, after a cruel twist of fate left him penniless, he, his wife and children were forced out of their beautiful home.

With nothing but holes in his pockets, Jeff had no alternative but to go back down the markets and start all over again. Did he still have what it took? Could he really get back everything he had lost?

A Pocketful of Holes and Dreams is the heartwarming true story of a little boy who had nothing but gained everything and proof that, sometimes, rags can be turned into riches . . .

ANGIE BEASLEY

THE FROG PRINCESS

From ugly duckling to beauty queen, this is the touching true tale of how a girl from Grimsby reached the stars.

Life didn't hold much promise for ordinary little Angie. With few jobs around, bland food and cold weather, the best that Angie could hope for was a job at the local Findus factory.

Her family didn't have it easy. Her baby brother was a cot death and the tragedy caused her mother to turn to the Jehovah's Witness faith. Their poverty, now combined with an austere belief system, meant no Christmas, no birthdays and little joy.

But aged 16, Angie decided that she was destined for bigger things. After seeing a TV advertisement she entered a beauty pageant. And won. She went on to take 25 titles, including Miss Leeds, and her home town title Miss Cleethorpes, giving her the opportunity to model while travelling the world.

Just as Angie felt that life couldn't get any better, she got engaged to a man who trapped her in a terrifying cycle of domestic violence. When she eventually escaped him, she had lost all of her money and self-esteem. She was on the bottom rung of the ladder yet again. But Angie picked herself up, turned her talents to event management and grafted her way to becoming Director of Miss England.

Evoking the magical, lost world of the 1970s beauty pageant, Angie's story is a real life fairytale with heart and humour.

read more   🄿

CHRISTINE MARION FRASER

BLUE ABOVE THE CHIMNEY

The wild childhood of a Glasgow tenement urchin

Born during the Second World War in Glasgow, Christine Fraser was her mother's eighth child. Growing up with her siblings in a tiny flat, learning to avoid her hardworking, hard-drinking one-eyed father, making a menace of herself in the streets along with the other urchins, Christine lived an impoverished life but never once cared. Until she was struck down by a terrible illness.

Suddenly, her wild days of childhood were over. A long spell in hospital completely changed her life. Now she found herself dependent on others for so many of her needs. And on top of that her mother and father died.

Yet Christine was always resourceful and never once looked down. She knew that always there, if you looked hard enough, was some blue up above the chimneys.

www.penguin.com

He just wanted a decent book to read ...

Not too much to ask, is it? It was in 1935 when Allen Lane, Managing Director of Bodley Head Publishers, stood on a platform at Exeter railway station looking for something good to read on his journey back to London. His choice was limited to popular magazines and poor-quality paperbacks – the same choice faced every day by the vast majority of readers, few of whom could afford hardbacks. Lane's disappointment and subsequent anger at the range of books generally available led him to found a company – and change the world.

'We believed in the existence in this country of a vast reading public for intelligent books at a low price, and staked everything on it'
Sir Allen Lane, 1902–1970, founder of Penguin Books

The quality paperback had arrived – and not just in bookshops. Lane was adamant that his Penguins should appear in chain stores and tobacconists, and should cost no more than a packet of cigarettes.

Reading habits (and cigarette prices) have changed since 1935, but Penguin still believes in publishing the best books for everybody to enjoy. We still believe that good design costs no more than bad design, and we still believe that quality books published passionately and responsibly make the world a better place.

So wherever you see the little bird – whether it's on a piece of prize-winning literary fiction or a celebrity autobiography, political tour de force or historical masterpiece, a serial-killer thriller, reference book, world classic or a piece of pure escapism – you can bet that it represents the very best that the genre has to offer.

Whatever you like to read – trust Penguin.